THE MERCHANT OF VENICE

THE MERCHANT OF VENICE

William Shakespeare

WORDSWORTH CLASSICS

The paper in this book is produced from pure wood
pulp, without the use of chlorine or any other substance
harmful to the environment. The energy used in its
production consists almost entirely of hydroelectricity
and heat generated from waste materials, thereby
conserving fossil fuels and contributing little to the
greenhouse effect.

This edition published 1994 by
Wordsworth Editions Limited
Cumberland House, Crib Street, Ware,
Hertfordshire SG12 9ET

Reprinted 1994

ISBN 1 85326 600 6

Printed and bound in Denmark by Nørhaven
Typeset in the UK by The R & B Partnership

INTRODUCTION

The Merchant of Venice was written between 1596 and 1598, first published in 1600 and this text was reprinted in the First Folio of 1623. It has several sources; Fiorentino's *Il Pecorone* (The Blockhead) of 1558, the *Gesta Romanorum* (1492) and Munday's *Zelauto*. Although the play is generally described as a comedy, and indeed much of it consists of light fantasy and courtly romance, there is an underlying plot of considerable moral dimension in the development of Shylock's character. Although there are some superficial parallels between Shylock and *Twelfth Night's* (1600) Malvolio, Shylock is altogether more sombre.

Bassanio, a poor but noble Venetian, borrows 3,000 ducats from his friend, the merchant Antonio, in order to finance his courting of the heiress Portia. Because Antonio's wealth is tied up in mercantile expeditions, he borrows the money from the Jew Shylock, who he has often berated for his extortionate interest rates. Shylock agrees to a three month loan, but attaches the macabre condition that if the money is not repaid at the end of this period, Antonio must forfeit a pound of his living flesh to be selected by Shylock from any part of his body. Bassanio woos, wins and weds the lovely Portia, his friend Gratiano marries Portia's maid Nerissa, and all seems well until the news arrives that all Antonio's ships have been lost at sea. Warned that Shylock intends to claim his pound of flesh, Portia who appreciates the love her new husband bears Antonio, takes legal instruction.

Disguised as the young Doctor of Law, Balthazar, she presents herself and Nerissa, disguised as a clerk, to the Duke of Venice's court to try the case. Shylock refuses to accept three times the original sum from the newly enriched Bassanio and insists on adhering to the original agreement. As Shylock prepares to cut, Portia points out that the contract makes no mention of blood, and that if one drop is spilt Shylock's goods and lands are forfeit to the state. Pursuing her advantage, she maintains that his life is forfeit for conspiring against the life of a Venetian citizen. The Duke spares Shylock's life, but gives half his property to Antonio, who returns it to Shylock on condition that he leaves it to his daughter Jessica who has secretly married Lorenzo another friend of Bassanio, and that he converts to Christianity.

The minor characters in the play are portrayed with all the concise wit and skill at Shakespeare's command. But the three main characters are remarkable for being quite untypical of normal Elizabethan values. Antonio, who should be the noble hero of the piece is portrayed as a self-righteous prig; Portia who might be expected to be a timid and loving heiress is in fact shown as an archetypal strong-minded woman, both feminine and feminist, while Shylock is presented a a tragic outsider. When one considers that the play was written in an age of extraordinary religious intolerance, it is remarkable that Shakespeare wrote Shylock's part as one of perverted nobility. The anachronistic political correctitude of the late twentieth century may find fault with *The Merchant of Venice*, but the intelligent reader will delight in the text almost as much as in the performance of the play.

Details of William Shakespeare's early life are scanty. He was the son of a prosperous merchant of Stratford upon Avon, and tradition has it that he was born on 23rd April 1564; records show that he was baptized three days later. It is likely that he attended the local Grammar School, but he had no university education. Of his early career there is no record, though John Aubrey states that he was a country schoolmaster. How he became involved with the stage is equally uncertain, but he was sufficiently established as a playwright by 1592 to be critized in print. He was leading member of the Lord Chamberlain's Company, which became the King's Men on the accession of James I in 1603. Shakespeare married Anne Hathaway in 1582, by whom he had two daughters and a son, Hamnet, who died in 1586. Towards the end of his life he loosened his ties with London, and retired to New Place, his substantial property in Stratford which he bought in 1597. He died on 23rd April 1616 aged 52, and is buried in Holy Trinity Church, Stratford.

Further reading:
R Berry: Shakespeare's Comedies: Explorations in Form 1972
W W Lawrence: Shakespeare's Problem Comedies 1931, 1969
B W Mowat: The Dramaturgy of Shakespeare's Romances 1976
E C Pettet: Shakespeare and the Romantic Tradition 1949, 1970
P G Philias: Shakespeare's Romantic Comedies 1966

THE MERCHANT OF VENICE

The scene: Venice, and
Portia's house at Belmont

CHARACTERS IN THE PLAY

The Duke of Venice

The Prince of Morocco
The Prince of Arragon } *suitors to Portia*

ANTONIO, *a Merchant of Venice*

BASSANIO, *his friend, suitor to Portia*

GRATIANO
SOLANIO } *friends to Antonio and Bassanio*
SALERIO

LORENZO, *in love with Jessica*

SHYLOCK, *a Jew*

TUBAL, *another Jew, friend to Shylock*

LANCELOT GOBBO, *a clown, servant to Shylock*

OLD GOBBO, *father to Lancelot*

LEONARDO, *servant to Bassanio*

BALTHAZAR
STEPHANO } *servants to Portia*

PORTIA, *a lady of Belmont*

NERISSA, *her waiting-maid*

JESSICA, *daughter to Shylock*

Magnificoes of Venice, officers of the Court of Justice,
a gaoler, servants, and other attendants

THE MERCHANT OF VENICE

*ANTONIO, SALERIO, and SOLANIO approach,
talking together*

Antonio. In sooth I know not why I am so sad,
It wearies me, you say it wearies you;
But how I caught it, found it, or came by it,
What stuff 'tis made of, whereof it is born,
I am to learn:
And such a want-wit sadness makes of me,
That I have much ado to know myself.

Salerio. Your mind is tossing on the ocean,
There, where your argosies with portly sail—
Like signiors and rich burghers on the flood,
Or as it were the pageants of the sea—
Do overpeer the petty traffickers,
That curtsy to them, do them reverence,
As they fly by them with their woven wings.

Solanio. Believe me, sir, had I such venture forth,
The better part of my affections would
Be with my hopes abroad. I should be still
Plucking the grass to know where sits the wind,
Piring in maps for ports and piers and roads:
And every object that might make me fear
Misfortune to my ventures, out of doubt,
Would make me sad.

Salerio.   My wind, cooling my broth,
Would blow me to an ague when I thought
What harm a wind too great might do at sea.
I should not see the sandy hour-glass run
But I should think of shallows and of flats,

And see my wealthy Andrew docked in sand,
Vailing her high-top lower than her ribs
To kiss her burial...Should I go to church
And see the holy edifice of stone,
And not bethink me straight of dangerous rocks,
Which touching but my gentle vessel's side
Would scatter all her spices on the stream,
Enrobe the roaring waters with my silks,
And, in a word, but even now worth this,
And now worth nothing? Shall I have the thought
To think on this, and shall I lack the thought
That such a thing bechanced would make me sad?
But tell not me—I know Antonio
Is sad to think upon his merchandise.

 Antonio. Believe me, no—I thank my fortune for it—
My ventures are not in one bottom trusted,
Nor to one place; nor is my whole estate
Upon the fortune of this present year:
Therefore my merchandise makes me not sad.

 Solanio. Why then you are in love.

 Antonio.   Fie, fie!

 Solanio. Not in love neither? then let us say you are sad
Because you are not merry; and 'twere as easy
For you to laugh and leap, and say you are merry,
Because you are not sad. Now, by two-headed Janus,
Nature hath framed strange fellows in her time:
Some that will evermore peep through their eyes,
And laugh like parrots at a bag-piper;
And other of such vinegar aspect,
That they'll not show their teeth in way of smile,
Though Nestor swear the jest be laughable....

BASSANIO, LORENZO, and GRATIANO are seen approaching

Here comes Bassanio, your most noble kinsman,

Gratiano, and Lorenzo....Fare ye well,
We leave you now with better company.
  Salerio. I would have stayed till I had made you merry,
If worthier friends had not prevented me.
  Antonio. Your worth is very dear in my regard.
I take it your own business calls on you,
And you embrace th'occasion to depart.
  Salerio. Good morrow, my good lords.
  Bassanio [*coming up*]. Good signiors both, when shall
    we laugh? say when?
You grow exceeding strange: must it be so?
  Salerio. We'll make our leisures to attend on yours.
                    [*Salerio and Solanio bow and depart*
  Lorenzo. My Lord Bassanio, since you have
    found Antonio,
We two will leave you, but at dinner-time
I pray you have in mind where we must meet.
  Bassanio. I will not fail you.
  Gratiano. You look not well, Signior Antonio,
You have too much respect upon the world:
They lose it that do buy it with much care,
Believe me you are marvellously changed.
  Antonio. I hold the world but as the world, Gratiano—
A stage, where every man must play a part,
And mine a sad one.
  Gratiano.   Let me play the fool,
With mirth and laughter let old wrinkles come,
And let my liver rather heat with wine,
Than my heart cool with mortifying groans.
Why should a man, whose blood is warm within,
Sit like his grandsire cut in alabaster?
Sleep when he wakes? and creep into the jaundice
By being peevish? I tell thee what, Antonio—
I love thee, and it is my love that speaks—

There are a sort of men whose visages
Do cream and mantle like a standing pond,
And do a wilful stillness entertain,
With purpose to be dressed in an opinion
Of wisdom, gravity, profound conceit,
As who should say, 'I am Sir Oracle,
And when I ope my lips let no dog bark'....
O, my Antonio, I do know of these
That therefore only are reputed wise
For saying nothing...when, I am very sure,
If they should speak, would almost damn those ears
Which, hearing them, would call their brothers fools.
I'll tell thee more of this another time.
But fish not with this melancholy bait
For this fool gudgeon, this opinion...
Come, good Lorenzo. Fare ye well awhile,
I'll end my exhortation after dinner.

Lorenzo. Well, we will leave you then till dinner-time.
I must be one of these same dumb wise men,
For Gratiano never lets me speak.

Gratiano. Well, keep me company but two years mo,
Thou shalt not know the sound of thine own tongue.

Antonio. Fare you well. I'll grow a talker for
   this gear.

Gratiano. Thanks, i'faith—for silence is only
   commendable
In a neat's tongue dried, and a maid not vendible.

   [*Gratiano and Lorenzo go off laughing, arm-in-arm*
Antonio. Is that any thing now?

Bassanio. Gratiano speaks an infinite deal of nothing,
more than any man in all Venice. His reasons are as
two grains of wheat hid in two bushels of chaff: you
shall seek all day ere you find them, and when you
have them they are not worth the search.

Antonio. Well, tell me now what lady is the same
To whom you swore a secret pilgrimage,
That you to-day promised to tell me of?

Bassanio. 'Tis not unknown to you, Antonio,
How much I have disabled mine estate,
By something showing a more swelling port
Than my faint means would grant continuance:
Nor do I now make moan to be abridged
From such a noble rate, but my chief care
Is to come fairly off from the great debts
Wherein my time, something too prodigal,
Hath left me gaged...To you, Antonio,
I owe the most in money and in love,
And from your love I have a warranty
To unburthen all my plots and purposes
How to get clear of all the debts I owe.

Antonio. I pray you, good Bassanio, let me know it,
And if it stand, as you yourself still do,
Within the eye of honour, be assured,
My purse, my person, my extremest means,
Lie all unlocked to your occasions.

Bassanio. In my school-days, when I had lost one shaft,
I shot his fellow of the self-same flight
The self-same way, with more advisèd watch,
To find the other forth, and by adventuring both,
I oft found both: I urge this childhood proof,
Because what follows is pure innocence....
I owe you much, and, like a wilful youth,
That which I owe is lost—but if you please
To shoot another arrow that self way
Which you did shoot the first, I do not doubt,
As I will watch the aim, or to find both,
Or bring your latter hazard back again,
And thankfully rest debtor for the first.

Antonio. You know me well, and herein spend but time
To wind about my love with circumstance,
And out of doubt you do me now more wrong
In making question of my uttermost
Than if you had made waste of all I have:
Then do but say to me what I should do
That in your knowledge may by me be done,
And I am prest unto it: therefore, speak.

Bassanio. In Belmont is a lady richly left,
And she is fair, and, fairer than that word,
Of wondrous virtues—sometimes from her eyes
I did receive fair speechless messages...
Her name is Portia, nothing undervalued
To Cato's daughter, Brutus' Portia—
Nor is the wide world ignorant of her worth,
For the four winds blow in from every coast
Renownéd suitors, and her sunny locks
Hang on her temples like a golden fleece,
Which makes her seat of Belmont Colchos' strand,
And many Jasons come in quest of her....
O my Antonio, had I but the means
To hold a rival place with one of them,
I have a mind presages me such thrift,
That I should questionless be fortunate.

Antonio. Thou know'st that all my fortunes are at sea,
Neither have I money nor commodity
To raise a present sum, therefore go forth,
Try what my credit can in Venice do—
That shall be racked, even to the uttermost,
To furnish thee to Belmont, to fair Portia....
Go, presently inquire, and so will I,
Where money is, and I no question make
To have it of my trust or for my sake.   [*they go*

[1.2.] *The hall of Portia's house at Belmont; at the back a gallery and beneath it the entrance to an alcove concealed by a curtain*

PORTIA *and her waiting-woman* NERISSA

Portia. By my troth, Nerissa, my little body is aweary of this great world.

Nerissa. You would be, sweet madam, if your miseries were in the same abundance as your good fortunes are: and yet for aught I see, they are as sick that surfeit with too much as they that starve with nothing; it is no mean happiness therefore to be seated in the mean—superfluity comes sooner by white hairs, but competency lives longer.

Portia. Good sentences, and well pronounced.

Nerissa. They would be better if well followed.

Portia. If to do were as easy as to know what were good to do, chapels had been churches, and poor men's cottages princes' palaces. It is a good divine that follows his own instructions. I can easier teach twenty what were good to be done, than be one of the twenty to follow mine own teaching...The brain may devise laws for the blood, but a hot temper leaps o'er a cold decree—such a hare is madness the youth, to skip o'er the meshes of good counsel the cripple...But this reasoning is not in the fashion to choose me a husband. O me, the word 'choose'! I may neither choose whom I would nor refuse whom I dislike—so is the will of a living daughter curbed by the will of a dead father... Is it not hard, Nerissa, that I cannot choose one, nor refuse none?

Nerissa. Your father was ever virtuous, and holy men at their death have good inspirations, therefore the lottery that he hath devised in these three chests of gold, silver and lead, whereof who chooses his meaning chooses you, will no doubt never be chosen by any rightly, but one whom you shall rightly love...But what warmth is there in your affection towards any of these princely suitors that are already come?

Portia. I pray thee over-name them, and as thou namest them, I will describe them, and according to my description level at my affection.

Nerissa. First there is the Neapolitan prince.

Portia. Ay, that's a colt indeed, for he doth nothing but talk of his horse, and he makes it a great appropriation to his own good parts that he can shoe him himself: I am much afeard my lady his mother played false with a smith.

Nerissa. Then is there the County Palatine.

Portia. He doth nothing but frown, as who should say, 'An you will not have me, choose!' He hears merry tales, and smiles not. I fear he will prove the weeping philosopher when he grows old, being so full of unmannerly sadness in his youth....I had rather be married to a death's-head with a bone in his mouth than to either of these: God defend me from these two!

Nerissa. How say you by the French lord, Monsieur Le Bon?

Portia. God made him, and therefore let him pass for a man—In truth, I know it is a sin to be a mocker, but he! why, he hath a horse better than the Neapolitan's, a better bad habit of frowning than the Count Palatine—he is every man in no man—if a throstle sing, he falls straight a cap'ring—he will fence with his own shadow. If I should marry him, I should marry twenty husbands...If he would despise me I would forgive him, for if he love me to madness, I shall never requite him.

Nerissa. What say you then to Falconbridge, the young baron of England?

Portia. You know I say nothing to him, for he understands not me, nor I him: he hath neither Latin, French, nor Italian, and you will come into the court and swear that I have a poor pennyworth in the English...He is a proper man's picture, but, alas! who can converse with a dumb-show? How oddly he is suited! I think he bought his doublet in Italy, his round hose in France, his bonnet in Germany, and his behaviour every where.

Nerissa. What think you of the Scottish lord, his neighbour?

Portia. That he hath a neighbourly charity in him, for he borrowed a box of the ear of the Englishman, and swore he would pay him again when he was able: I think the Frenchman became his surety, and sealed under for another.

Nerissa. How like you the young German, the Duke of Saxony's nephew?

Portia. Very vilely in the morning when he is sober, and most vilely in the afternoon when he is drunk: when he is best, he is a little worse than a man, and when he is worst, he is little better than a beast—an the worst fall that ever fell, I hope I shall make shift to go without him.

Nerissa. If he should offer to choose, and choose the right casket, you should refuse to perform your father's will, if you should refuse to accept him.

Portia. Therefore, for fear of the worst, I pray thee set a deep glass of rhenish wine on the contrary casket, for if the devil be within, and that temptation without, I know he will choose it....I will do any thing, Nerissa, ere I will be married to a sponge.

Nerissa. You need not fear, lady, the having any of these lords—they have acquainted me with their determinations, which is indeed to return to their home, and to trouble you with no more suit, unless you may be won by some other sort than your father's imposition depending on the caskets.

Portia. If I live to be as old as Sibylla, I will die as chaste as Diana, unless I be obtained by the manner of my father's will: I am glad this parcel of wooers are so reasonable, for there is not one among them but I dote on his very absence: and I pray God grant them a fair departure.

Nerissa. Do you not remember, lady, in your father's time, a Venetian, a scholar and a soldier, that came hither in company of the Marquis of Montferrat?

Portia. Yes, yes, it was Bassanio, as I think so was he called.

Nerissa. True, madam, he, of all the men that ever my foolish eyes looked upon, was the best deserving a fair lady.

Portia. I remember him well, and I remember him worthy of thy praise....

A servant enters

How now! what news?

Servant. The four strangers seek for you, madam, to take their leave: and there is a forerunner come from a fifth, the Prince of Morocco, who brings word the prince his master will be here to-night.

Portia. If I could bid the fifth welcome with so good heart as I can bid the other four farewell, I should be glad of his approach: if he have the condition of a saint, and the complexion of a devil, I had rather he should shrive me than wive me.... Come, Nerissa. Sirrah, go before:
Whiles we shut the gate upon one wooer, another
      knocks at the door.   [*they go out*

[1.3.] *A street in Venice, before Shylock's house*

BASSANIO *and* SHYLOCK

Shylock. Three thousand ducats—well.

Bassanio. Ay, sir, for three months.

Shylock. For three months—well.

Bassanio. For the which, as I told you, Antonio shall be bound.

Shylock. Antonio shall become bound—well.

Bassanio. May you stead me? Will you pleasure me? Shall I know your answer?

Shylock. Three thousand ducats for three months—and Antonio bound.

Bassanio. Your answer to that.

Shylock. Antonio is a good man.

Bassanio. Have you heard any imputation to the contrary?

Shylock. Ho no, no, no, no...my meaning in saying he is a good man, is to have you understand me that he is sufficient. Yet his means are in supposition...He hath an argosy bound to Tripolis, another to the Indies— I understand moreover upon the Rialto, he hath a third at Mexico, a fourth for England, and other ventures he hath squandered abroad. But ships are but boards, sailors but men—there be land-rats and water-rats, land-thieves and water-thieves—I mean pirates—and then there is the peril of waters, winds, and rocks...The man is, notwithstanding, sufficient. Three thousand ducats—I think I may take his bond.

Bassanio. Be assured you may.

Shylock. I will be assured I may: and, that I may be assured, I will bethink me—may I speak with Antonio?

Bassanio. If it please you to dine with us.

(*Shylock.* Yes, to smell pork, to eat of the habitation

which your prophet the Nazarite conjured the devil
into...I will buy with you, sell with you, talk with you,
walk with you, and so following: but I will not eat with
you, drink with you, nor pray with you....[*aloud*] What
news on the Rialto? Who is he comes here?

ANTONIO approaches

Bassanio. This is Signior Antonio.
[*he draws Antonio aside*

(*Shylock*. How like a fawning publican he looks!
I hate him for he is a Christian:
But more for that in low simplicity
He lends out money gratis, and brings down
The rate of usance here with us in Venice....
If I can catch him once upon the hip,
I will feed fat the ancient grudge I bear him....
He hates our sacred nation, and he rails,
Even there where merchants most do congregate,
On me, my bargains, and my well-won thrift,
Which he calls interest...Curséd be my tribe,
If I forgive him!

Bassanio [*turns*].   Shylock, do you hear?

Shylock. I am debating of my present store,
And by the near guess of my memory
I cannot instantly raise up the gross
Of full three thousand ducats: what of that?
Tubal a wealthy Hebrew of my tribe
Will furnish me; but soft—how many months
Do you desire? [*bows to Antonio*] Rest you fair, good
    signior,
Your worship was the last man in our mouths.

Antonio. Shylock, albeit I neither lend nor borrow
By taking nor by giving of excess,
Yet to supply the ripe wants of my friend

I'll break a custom...[*to Bassanio*] Is he yet possessed
How much ye would?
  Shylock.   Ay, ay, three thousand ducats.
  Antonio. And for three months.
  Shylock. I had forgot—three months—you told me so....
Well then, your bond: and let me see—but hear you,
Methought you said you neither lend nor borrow
Upon advantage.
  Antonio.   I do never use it.
  Shylock. When Jacob grazed his uncle Laban's sheep,
This Jacob from our holy Abram was
(As his wise mother wrought in his behalf)
The third possessor; ay, he was the third—
  Antonio. And what of him? did he take interest?
  Shylock. No, not take interest—not as you would say
Directly interest—mark what Jacob did.
When Laban and himself were compromised
That all the eanlings which were streaked and pied
Should fall as Jacob's hire, the ewes, being rank
In end of autumn, turnéd to the rams,
And when the work of generation was
Between these woolly breeders in the act,
The skilful shepherd pilled me certain wands,
And, in the doing of the deed of kind,
He stuck them up before the fulsome ewes,
Who, then conceiving, did in eaning time
Fall parti-coloured lambs, and those were Jacob's....
This was a way to thrive, and he was blest:
And thrift is blessing if men steal it not.
  Antonio. This was a venture, sir, that Jacob served for—
A thing not in his power to bring to pass,
But swayed and fashioned by the hand of heaven....
Was this inserted to make interest good?
Or is your gold and silver ewes and rams?

Shylock. I cannot tell, I make it breed as fast—
But note me, signior.
    Antonio.   Mark you this, Bassanio,
The devil can cite Scripture for his purpose.
An evil soul, producing holy witness,
Is like a villain with a smiling cheek,
A goodly apple rotten at the heart....
O, what a goodly outside falsehood hath!
  Shylock. Three thousand ducats—'tis a good
      round sum....
Three months from twelve, then let me see the rate.
  Antonio. Well, Shylock, shall we be beholding to you?
  Shylock. Signior Antonio, many a time and oft
In the Rialto you have rated me
About my moneys and my usances:
Still have I borne it with a patient shrug,
For suff'rance is the badge of all our tribe.
You call me misbeliever, cut-throat dog,
And spet upon my Jewish gaberdine,
And all for use of that which is mine own....
Well then, it now appears you need my help:
Go to then, you come to me, and you say,
'Shylock, we would have moneys'—you say so!
You that did void your rheum upon my beard,
And foot me as you spurn a stranger cur
Over your threshold—moneys is your suit.
What should I say to you? Should I not say
'Hath a dog money? is it possible
A cur can lend three thousand ducats?' or
Shall I bend low, and in a bondman's key,
With bated breath, and whisp'ring humbleness,
Say this:
'Fair sir, you spet on me on Wednesday last—
You spurned me such a day—another time

You called me dog: and for these courtesies
I'll lend you thus much moneys'?

Antonio. I am as like to call thee so again,
To spet on thee again, to spurn thee too.
If thou wilt lend this money, lend it not
As to thy friends—for when did friendship take
A breed for barren metal of his friend?—
But lend it rather to thine enemy,
Who if he break, thou mayst with better face
Exact the penalty.

Shylock. Why, look you, how you storm!
I would be friends with you, and have your love,
Forget the shames that you have stained me with,
Supply your present wants, and take no doit
Of usance for my moneys, and you'll not hear me:
This is kind I offer.

Antonio. This were kindness.

Shylock. This kindness will I show.
Go with me to a notary, seal me there
Your single bond, and, in a merry sport,
If you repay me not on such a day,
In such a place, such sum or sums as are
Expressed in the condition, let the forfeit
Be nominated for an equal pound
Of your fair flesh, to be cut off and taken
In what part of your body pleaseth me.

Antonio. Content, in faith—I'll seal to such a bond,
And say there is much kindness in the Jew.

Bassanio. You shall not seal to such a bond for me,
I'll rather dwell in my necessity.

Antonio. Why, fear not man, I will not forfeit it.
Within these two months, that's a month before
This bond expires, I do expect return
Of thrice three times the value of this bond.

Shylock. O father Abram! what these Christians are,
Whose own hard dealing teaches them suspect
The thoughts of others...Pray you, tell me this—
If he should break his day, what should I gain
By the exaction of the forfeiture?
A pound of man's flesh, taken from a man,
Is not so estimable, profitable neither
As flesh of muttons, beefs, or goats say.
To buy his favour, I extend this .endship.
If he will take it, so—if not, adi ..,
And, for my love, I pray you vrong me not.
  Antonio. Yes, Shylock, I will seal unto this bond.
  Shylock. Then meet me forthwith at the notary's,
Give him direction for this merry bond,
And I will go and purse the ducats straight,
See to my house left in the fearful guard
Of an unthrifty knave; and presently
I will be with you.
  Antonio.   Hie thee, gentle Jew....
                              [*Shylock enters his house*
The Hebrew will turn Christian—he grows kind.
  Bassanio. I like not fair terms and a villain's mind.
  Antonio. Come on—in this there can be no dismay,
My ships come home a month before the day.
                              [*they walk away*

[2.1.]   *The hall of Portia's house at Belmont*

Enter the Prince of MOROCCO, '*a tawny Moor all in
white, and three or four followers accordingly, with*
PORTIA, NERISSA, *and their train*'

  Morocco. Mislike me not for my complexion,
The shadowed livery of the burnished sun,
To whom I am a neighbour and near bred.

Bring me the fairest creature northward born,
Where Phœbus' fire scarce thaws the icicles,
And let us make incision for your love,
To prove whose blood is reddest, his or mine.
I tell thee, lady, this aspéct of mine
Hath feared the valiant. By my love, I swear
The best-regarded virgins of our clime
Have loved it too...I would not change this hue,
Except to steal your thoughts, my gentle queen.
   Portia. In terms of choice I am not solely led
By nice direction of a maiden's eyes:
Besides, the lott'ry of my destiny
Bars me the right of voluntary choosing:
But if my father had not scanted me
And hedged me by his wit, to yield myself
His wife who wins me by that means I told you,
Yourself, renownéd prince, then stood as fair
As any comer I have looked on yet
For my affection.
   Morocco.   Even for that I thank you.
Therefore, I pray you, lead me to the caskets
To try my fortune...By this scimitar—
That slew the Sophy and a Persian prince
That won three fields of Sultan Solyman—
I would o'erstare the sternest eyes that look:
Outbrave the heart most daring on the earth:
Pluck the young sucking cubs from the she-bear,
Yea, mock the lion when a' roars for prey,
To win thee, lady....But, alas the while!
If Hercules and Lichas play at dice
Which is the better man, the greater throw
May turn by fortune from the weaker hand:
†So is Alcides beaten by his wag,
And so may I, blind fortune leading me,

Miss that which one unworthier may attain,
And die with grieving.

Portia.   You must take your chance—
And either not attempt to choose at all,
Or swear, before you choose, if you choose wrong,
Never to speak to lady afterward
In way of marriage. Therefore be advised.

Morocco. Nor will not. Come, bring me unto my chance.

Portia. First, forward to the temple. After dinner
Your hazard shall be made.

Morocco.   Good fortune then!
To make me blest or cursed'st among men.   [*they go*

[2. 2.]   *The street before Shylock's house*

LANCELOT GOBBO *comes forth, scratching his head*

Lancelot. Certainly my conscience will serve me to
run from this Jew my master...The fiend is at mine
elbow, and tempts me, saying to me, 'Gobbo, Lancelot
Gobbo, good Lancelot,' or 'good Gobbo,' or 'good
Lancelot Gobbo, use your legs, take the start, run
away.' My conscience says, 'No; take heed honest
Lancelot, take heed honest Gobbo,' or as aforesaid,
'honest Lancelot Gobbo, do not run, scorn running
with thy heels'...Well, the most courageous fiend bids
me pack. 'Fia!' says the fiend, 'away!' says the fiend,
'for the heavens, rouse up a brave mind,' says the fiend,
'and run'...Well, my conscience, hanging about the
neck of my heart, says very wisely to me: 'My honest
friend, Lancelot, being an honest man's son,'—or rather
an honest woman's son—for indeed my father did something smack, something grow to; he had a kind of
taste; well, my conscience says, 'Lancelot, budge not.'
'Budge,' says the fiend. 'Budge not,' says my con-

science. 'Conscience,' say I, 'you counsel well.'
'Fiend,' say I, 'you counsel well.' To be ruled by my
conscience, I should stay with the Jew my master, who
(God bless the mark!) is a kind of devil; and to run
away from the Jew, I should be ruled by the fiend, who,
saving your reverence, is the devil himself...Certainly,
the Jew is the very devil incarnation—and, in my conscience, my conscience is but a kind of hard conscience,
to offer to counsel me to stay with the Jew...The fiend
gives the more friendly counsel...I will run, fiend. My
heels are at your commandment, I will run.

He runs, and stumbles into the arms of Old GOBBO,
who comes along the street 'with a basket'

Old Gobbo [*gasps*]. Master young-man, you I pray
you, which is the way to Master Jew's?

Lancelot. O heavens, this is my true-begotten father,
who being more than sand-blind, high gravel-blind,
knows me not. I will try confusions with him.

Old Gobbo. Master, young gentleman, I pray you
which is the way to Master Jew's?

Lancelot [*shouts in his ear*]. Turn up on your right
hand at the next turning, but at the next turning of all
on your left; marry at the very next turning turn of no
hand, but turn down indirectly to the Jew's house.

Old Gobbo. Be God's sonties, 'twill be a hard way to
hit. Can you tell me whether one Lancelot that dwells
with him, dwell with him or no?

Lancelot. Talk you of young Master Lancelot?—
[*aside*] Mark me now, now will I raise the waters...
Talk you of young Master Lancelot?

Old Gobbo. No 'master,' sir, but a poor man's son.
His father, though I say't, is an honest exceeding poor
man, and God be thanked well to live.

Lancelot. Well, let his father be what a' will, we talk of young Master Lancelot.

Old Gobbo. Your worship's friend and Lancelot, sir.

Lancelot. But I pray you ergo old man, ergo I beseech you, talk you of young Master Lancelot.

Old Gobbo. Of Lancelot, an't please your mastership.

Lancelot. Ergo—Master Lancelot! Talk not of Master Lancelot, father, for the young gentleman—according to fates and destinies, and such odd sayings, the sisters three, and such branches of learning—is indeed deceased, or as you would say in plain terms, gone to heaven.

Old Gobbo. Marry, God forbid! the boy was the very staff of my age, my very prop.

(*Lancelot.* Do I look like a cudgel or a hovel-post, a staff or a prop?
Do you know me, father?

Old Gobbo. Alack the day, I know you not, young gentleman, but I pray you tell me, is my boy—God rest his soul!—alive or dead?

Lancelot. Do you not know me, father?

Old Gobbo. Alack, sir, I am sand-blind, I know you not.

Lancelot. Nay, indeed, if you had your eyes, you might fail of the knowing me: it is a wise father that knows his own child....[*he kneels*] Well, old man, I will tell you news of your son. Give me your blessing. Truth will come to light, murder cannot be hid long, a man's son may, but in the end truth will out.

Old Gobbo. Pray you, sir, stand up. I am sure you are not Lancelot, my boy.

Lancelot. Pray you let's have no more fooling about it, but give me your blessing: I am Lancelot, your boy that was, your son that is, your child that shall be.

Old Gobbo. I cannot think you are my son.

Lancelot. I know not what I shall think of that: but I am Lancelot, the Jew's man, and I am sure Margery, your wife, is my mother.

Old Gobbo. Her name is Margery, indeed. I'll be sworn, if thou be Lancelot, thou art mine own flesh and blood...[*he feels for Lancelot's face; Lancelot bows and presents the nape of his neck*] Lord worshipped might he be! what a beard hast thou got! thou hast got more hair on thy chin than Dobbin my fill-horse has on his tail.

Lancelot. It should seem then that Dobbin's tail grows backward. I am sure he had more hair of his tail than I have of my face, when I last saw him.

Old Gobbo. Lord, how art thou changed! How dost thou and thy master agree? I have brought him a present...How 'gree you now?

Lancelot. Well, well—but, for mine own part, as I have set up my rest to run away, so I will not rest till I have run some ground...My master's a very Jew—give him a present! give him a halter—I am famished in his service....you may tell every finger I have with my ribs...Father, I am glad you are come. Give me your present to one Master Bassanio, who indeed gives rare new liveries. If I serve not him, I will run as far as God has any ground....O rare fortune! here comes the man—to him, father, for I am a Jew if I serve the Jew any longer.

BASSANIO approaches with LEONARDO and other followers

Bassanio [*talking to a servant*]. You may do so, but let it be so hasted that supper be ready at the farthest by five of the clock...See these letters delivered, put the liveries to making, and desire Gratiano to come anon to my lodging. [*the servant goes*

Lancelot [*thrusting forward the old man*]. To him, father.

Old Gobbo [*bows*]. God bless your worship!

Bassanio. Gramercy, wouldst thou aught with me?

Old Gobbo. Here's my son, sir, a poor boy—

Lancelot [*comes forward himself*]. Not a poor boy, sir, but the rich Jew's man that would, sir, as my father shall specify— [*retreats behind his father*

Old Gobbo. He hath a great infection, sir, as one would say to serve—

Lancelot [*comes forward*]. Indeed the short and the long is, I serve the Jew, and have a desire as my father shall specify— [*retreats*

Old Gobbo. His master and he (saving your worship's reverence) are scarce cater-cousins—

Lancelot [*comes forward*]. To be brief, the very truth is, that the Jew having done me wrong, doth cause me as my father being I hope an old man shall frutify unto you— [*retreats*

Old Gobbo. I have here a dish of doves that I would bestow upon your worship, and my suit is—

Lancelot [*comes forward*]. In very brief, the suit is impertinent to myself, as your worship shall know by this honest old man, and though I say it, though old man, yet poor man, my father.

Bassanio. One speak for both. What would you?

Lancelot. Serve you, sir.

Old Gobbo. That is the very defect of the matter, sir.

Bassanio. I know thee well, thou hast obtained thy suit. Shylock, thy master, spoke with me this day, And hath preferred thee, if it be preferment To leave a rich Jew's service, to become The follower of so poor a gentleman.

Lancelot. The old proverb is very well parted

between my master Shylock and you, sir—you have
'the grace of God,' sir, and he hath 'enough.'

Bassanio. Thou speak'st it well; go, father, with
    thy son.
Take leave of thy old master, and inquire
My lodging out. [*to his followers*] Give him a livery
More guarded than his fellows': see it done.
                [*he talks with Leonardo apart*

Lancelot. Father, in. I cannot get a service, no!
I have ne'er a tongue in my head! Well...[*looking on his
palm*] if any man in Italy have a fairer table which doth
offer to swear upon a book I shall have good fortune...
Go to, here's a simple line of life, here's a small trifle
of wives—alas, fifteen wives is nothing, eleven widows,
and nine maids, is a simple coming-in for one man—
and then to scape drowning thrice, and to be in peril
of my life with the edge of a feather-bed. Here are simple
scapes...Well, if Fortune be a woman, she's a good
wench for this gear...Father, come. I'll take my leave
of the Jew in the twinkling.
        [*Lancelot and Old Gobbo enter Shylock's house*

Bassanio. I pray thee, good Leonardo, think on this.
These things being bought and orderly bestowed,
Return in haste, for I do feast to-night
My best-esteemed acquaintance. Hie thee, go.

Leonardo. My best endeavours shall be done herein.

      As he goes off he meets GRATIANO
        coming along the street

Gratiano. Where's your master?
Leonardo.   Yonder, sir, he walks.
                  [*Leonardo departs*

Gratiano. Signior Bassanio!
Bassanio.   Gratiano!

Gratiano. I have a suit to you.

Bassanio.   You have obtained it.

Gratiano. You must not deny me—I must go with you to Belmont.

Bassanio. Why, then you must. But hear thee Gratiano,
Thou art too wild, too rude, and bold of voice—
Parts that become thee happily enough,
And in such eyes as ours appear not faults;
But where thou art not known, why, there they show
Something too liberal. Pray thee, take pain
To allay with some cold drops of modesty
Thy skipping spirit, lest through thy wild behaviour
I be misconstrued in the place I go to,
And lose my hopes.

  Gratiano.   Signior Bassanio, hear me—
If I do not put on a sober habit,
Talk with respect, and swear but now and then,
Wear prayer-books in my pocket, look demurely,
Nay more, while grace is saying, hood mine eyes
Thus with my hat, and sigh, and say 'amen';
Use all the observance of civility,
Like one well studied in a sad ostent
To please his grandam, never trust me more.

  Bassanio. Well, we shall see your bearing.

  Gratiano. Nay, but I bar to-night, you shall not gauge me
By what we do to-night.

  Bassanio.   No, that were pity,
I would entreat you rather to put on
Your boldest suit of mirth, for we have friends
That purpose merriment...But fare you well,
I have some business.

  Gratiano. And I must to Lorenzo, and the rest.
But we will visit you at supper-time.

                                        [*they go their way*

[2. 3.] *The door opens: JESSICA and LANCELOT come forth*

Jessica. I am sorry thou wilt leave my father so—
Our house is hell, and thou, a merry devil,
Didst rob it of some taste of tediousness.
But fare thee well, there is a ducat for thee.
And, Lancelot, soon at supper shalt thou see
Lorenzo, who is thy new master's guest—
Give him this letter, do it secretly,
And so farewell: I would not have my father
See me talk with thee.

Lancelot. Adieu! tears exhibit my tongue. Most
beautiful pagan, most sweet Jew! if a Christian do not
play the knave and get thee, I am much deceived...But
adieu, these foolish drops do something drown my
manly spirit; adieu! [*he goes*

Jessica. Farewell, good Lancelot....
Alack, what heinous sin is it in me
To be ashamed to be my father's child!
But though I am a daughter to his blood,
I am not to his manners...O Lorenzo,
If thou keep promise, I shall end this strife,
Become a Christian, and thy loving wife. [*she goes within*

[2. 4.] *Another street in Venice*

GRATIANO, LORENZO, SALERIO and SOLANIO
in lively conversation

Lorenzo. Nay, we will slink away in supper-time,
Disguise us at my lodging, and return
All in an hour.

Gratiano. We have not made good preparation.

Salerio. We have not spoke as yet of torch-bearers.

Solanio. 'Tis vile, unless it may be quaintly ordered,
And better in my mind not undertook.

Lorenzo. 'Tis now but four o'clock—we have two hours
To furnish us...   LANCELOT *comes up*

Friend Lancelot, what's the news?
Lancelot [*takes a letter from his wallet*]. An it shall
please you to break up this, it shall seem to signify.
Lorenzo. I know the hand. In faith 'tis a fair hand,
And whiter than the paper it writ on,
Is the fair hand that writ.
Gratiano.   Love-news, in faith.
Lancelot. By your leave, sir.
Lorenzo. Whither goest thou?
Lancelot. Marry, sir, to bid my old master the Jew
to sup to-night with my new master the Christian.
Lorenzo. Hold here, take this.   [*he gives him money*
                              Tell gentle Jessica
I will not fail her—speak it privately.   [*Lancelot goes*
Go, gentlemen,
Will you prepare you for this masque to-night?
I am provided of a torch-bearer.
Salerio. Ay, marry, I'll be gone about it straight.
Solanio. And so will I.
Lorenzo.   Meet me and Gratiano
At Gratiano's lodging some hour hence.
Salerio. 'Tis good we do so.
                    [*Salerio and Solanio leave them*
Gratiano. Was not that letter from fair Jessica?
Lorenzo. I must needs tell thee all. She hath directed
How I shall take her from her father's house,
What gold and jewels she is furnished with,
What page's suit she hath in readiness.
If e'er the Jew her father come to heaven
It will be for his gentle daughter's sake,
And never dare misfortune cross her foot

Unless she do it under this excuse—
That she is issue to a faithless Jew...
Come, go with me. Peruse this, as thou goest.
Fair Jessica shall be my torch-bearer.   [*they walk on*

[2. 5.]   *The street before Shylock's house*

          SHYLOCK *and* LANCELOT *come forth*

Shylock. Well, thou shalt see, thy eyes shall be
      thy judge,
The difference of old Shylock and Bassanio...
What, Jessica!—Thou shalt not gormandise,
As thou hast done with me...What, Jessica!—
And sleep and snore, and rend apparel out....
Why, Jessica, I say!
  Lancelot [*bawls*].   Why, Jessica!
  Shylock. Who bids thee call? I do not bid thee call.
  Lancelot. Your worship was wont to tell me I could
do nothing without bidding.

          JESSICA *appears at the door*

  Jessica. Call you? What is your will?
  Shylock. I am bid forth to supper, Jessica.
There are my keys...But wherefore should I go?
I am not bid for love—they flatter me.
But yet I'll go in hate, to feed upon
The prodigal Christian....Jessica, my girl,
Look to my house. I am right loath to go—
There is some ill a-brewing towards my rest,
For I did dream of money-bags to-night.
  Lancelot. I beseech you, sir, go. My young master
doth expect your reproach.
  Shylock. So do I his.
  Lancelot. And they have conspired together—I will

not say you shall see a masque, but if you do, then it
was not for nothing that my nose fell a-bleeding on
Black-Monday last, at six o'clock i'th' morning, falling
out that year on Ash-Wednesday was four year, in
th'afternoon.

Shylock. What, are there masques? Hear you me,
    Jessica—
Lock up my doors, and when you hear the drum
And the vile squealing of the wry-neck'd fife,
Clamber not you up to the casements then,
Nor thrust your head into the public street
To gaze on Christian fools with varnished faces:
But stop my house's ears, I mean my casements,
Let not the sound of shallow fopp'ry enter
My sober house....By Jacob's staff I swear
I have no mind of feasting forth to-night:
But I will go...Go you before me, sirrah—
Say I will come.

    Lancelot.   I will go before, sir....
        [*as he departs he passes by the door and whispers*
Mistress, look out at window, for all this—
        There will come a Christian by,
        Will be worth a Jewess' eye.   [*he goes*
Shylock. What says that fool of Hagar's offspring, ha?
Jessica. His words were, 'Farewell, mistress'—
    nothing else.
Shylock. The patch is kind enough, but a huge feeder,
Snail-slow in profit, and he sleeps by day
More than the wild-cat: drones hive not with me.
Therefore I part with him, and part with him
To one that I would have him help to waste
His borrowed purse....Well, Jessica, go in.
Perhaps I will return immediately.
Do as I bid you, shut doors after you.

Fast bind, fast find,
A proverb never stale in thrifty mind.   [*he goes*

   Jessica. Farewell—and if my fortune be not crost,
I have a father, you a daughter, lost.   [*she goes within*

[2.6.]   GRATIANO *and* SALERIO *come up,*
                    in masquing attire

   Gratiano. This is the pent-house, under which Lorenzo
Desired us to make stand.
   Salerio.   His hour is almost past.
   Gratiano. And it is marvel he out-dwells his hour,
For lovers ever run before the clock.
   Salerio. O, ten times faster Venus' pigeons fly
To seal love's bonds new-made, than they are wont
To keep obligéd faith unforfeited!
   Gratiano. That ever holds: who riseth from a feast
With that keen appetite that he sits down?
Where is the horse that doth untread again
His tedious measures with the unbated fire
That he did pace them first? All things that are,
Are with more spirit chaséd than enjoyed.
How like a younger or a prodigal
The scarféd bark puts from her native bay,
Hugged and embracéd by the strumpet wind!
How like the prodigal doth she return,
With over-weathered ribs and ragged sails,
Lean, rent and beggared by the strumpet wind!

            LORENZO *approaches in haste*

   Salerio. Here comes Lorenzo—more of this hereafter.
   Lorenzo. Sweet friends, your patience for my
        long abode.
Not I, but my affairs, have made you wait:
When you shall please to play the thieves for wives

I'll watch as long for you then....Approach.
Here dwells my father Jew....Ho! who's within?

*A casement window opens above the door
and JESSICA leans out, clad as a boy*

Jessica. Who are you? Tell me, for more certainty,
Albeit I'll swear that I do know your tongue.
  Lorenzo. Lorenzo, and thy love.
  Jessica. Lorenzo, certain, and my love indeed,
For who love I so much? And now who knows
But you, Lorenzo, whether I am yours?
  Lorenzo. Heaven and thy thoughts are witness
      that thou art.
  Jessica. Here, catch this casket, it is worth the pains....
                              [*she casts it down*
I am glad 'tis night, you do not look on me,
For I am much ashamed of my exchange:
But love is blind, and lovers cannot see
The pretty follies that themselves commit,
For if they could, Cupid himself would blush
To see me thus transforméd to a boy.
  Lorenzo. Descend, for you must be my torch-bearer.
  Jessica. What, must I hold a candle to my shames?
They in themselves, good sooth, are too too light.
Why, 'tis an office of discovery, love,
And I should be obscured.
  Lorenzo.   So are you, sweet,
Even in the lovely garnish of a boy.
But come at once,
For the close night doth play the runaway,
And we are stayed for at Bassanio's feast.
  Jessica. I will make fast the doors, and gild myself
With some mo ducats, and be with you straight.
                              [*she closes the casement*
  Gratiano. Now, by my hood, a gentle and no Jew.

Lorenzo. Beshrew me but I love her heartily,
For she is wise, if I can judge of her,
And fair she is, if that mine eyes be true,
And true she is, as she hath proved herself:
And therefore, like herself, wise, fair, and true,
Shall she be placéd in my constant soul....

    JESSICA comes from the house

What, art thou come? On, gentlemen, away—
Our masquing mates by this time for us stay.

    [*he departs with Jessica and Salerio*

    ANTONIO comes along the street

 Antonio. Who's there?
 Gratiano. Signior Antonio?
 Antonio. Fie, fie, Gratiano! where are all the rest?
'Tis nine o'clock—our friends all stay for you.
No masque to-night, the wind is come about,
Bassanio presently will go aboard.
I have sent twenty out to seek for you.
 Gratiano. I am glad on't. I desire no more delight
Than to be under sail and gone to-night.   [*they go*

[2.7.] *The hall of Portia's house at Belmont;* PORTIA
enters, with the Prince of MOROCCO, *and their trains*

 Portia. Go, draw aside the curtains, and discover
The several caskets to this noble prince...

  Servants draw back the curtains and reveal a table
    and three caskets thereon

Now make your choice. [*Morocco examines the caskets*
 Morocco. The first, of gold, who this inscription bears,
'Who chooseth me shall gain what many men desire'....
The second, silver, which this promise carries,
'Who chooseth me shall get as much as he deserves'....

This third, dull lead, with warning all as blunt,
'Who chooseth me must give and hazard all he hath'....
How shall I know if I do choose the right?

Portia. The one of them contains my picture, prince.
If you choose that, then I am yours withal.

Morocco. Some god direct my judgement! Let me see,
I will survey th'inscriptions back again.
What says this leaden casket?
'Who chooseth me must give and hazard all he hath.'
Must give—for what? for lead? hazard for lead?
This casket threatens. Men that hazard all
Do it in hope of fair advantages:
A golden mind stoops not to shows of dross.
I'll then nor give nor hazard aught for lead....
What says the silver with her virgin hue?
'Who chooseth me shall get as much as he deserves.'
As much as he deserves! Pause there, Morocco,
And weigh thy value with an even hand.
If thou be'st rated by thy estimation,
Thou dost deserve enough—and yet enough
May not extend so far as to the lady:
And yet to be afeard of my deserving
Were but a weak disabling of myself....
As much as I deserve! Why, that's the lady.
I do in birth deserve her, and in fortunes,
In graces, and in qualities of breeding:
But more than these, in love I do deserve.
What if I strayed no further, but chose here?
Let's see once more this saying graved in gold:
'Who chooseth me shall gain what many men desire'...
Why, that's the lady—all the world desires her.
From the four corners of the earth they come,
To kiss this shrine, this mortal-breathing saint.
The Hyrcanian deserts and the vasty wilds

Of wide Arabia are as throughfares now
For princes to come view fair Portia.
The watery kingdom, whose ambitious head
Spets in the face of heaven, is no bar
To stop the foreign spirits, but they come,
As o'er a brook, to see fair Portia....
One of these three contains her heavenly picture.
Is't like that lead contains her? 'Twere damnation
To think so base a thought—it were too gross
To rib her cerecloth in the obscure grave.
Or shall I think in silver she's immured,
Being ten times undervalued to tried gold?
O sinful thought! Never so rich a gem
Was set in worse than gold....They have in England
A coin that bears the figure of an angel
Stampéd in gold, but that's insculped upon;
But here an angel in a golden bed
Lies all within....Deliver me the key:
Here do I choose, and thrive I as I may!
  Portia. There, take it, prince, and if my form
    lie there,
Then I am yours.   *[he unlocks the golden casket*
  Morocco.   O hell! what have we here?
A carrion Death, within whose empty eye
There is a written scroll! I'll read the writing.
> 'All that glisters is not gold,
> Often have you heard that told.
> Many a man his life hath sold,
> But my outside to behold.
> Gilded tombs do worms infold...
> Had you been as wise as bold,
> Young in limbs, in judgement old,
> Your answer had not been inscrolled—
> Fare you well, your suit is cold.'

Cold, indeed, and labour lost.
Then, farewell heat, and welcome frost...
Portia, adieu! I have too grieved a heart
To take a tedious leave: thus losers part.

                           [he departs with his retinue

Portia. A gentle riddance. Draw the curtains, go.
Let all of his complexion choose me so.   *[they go out*

[2.8.]   *A street in Venice*

SALERIO *and* SOLANIO

Salerio. Why man, I saw Bassanio under sail,
With him is Gratiano gone along;
And in their ship I am sure Lorenzo is not.
  Solanio. The villain Jew with outcries raised the duke,
Who went with him to search Bassanio's ship.
  Salerio. He came too late, the ship was under sail,
But there the duke was given to understand
That in a gondola were seen together
Lorenzo and his amorous Jessica.
Besides, Antonio certified the duke
They were not with Bassanio in his ship.
  Solanio. I never heard a passion so confused,
So strange, outrageous, and so variable,
As the dog Jew did utter in the streets.
'My daughter! O my ducats! O my daughter!
Fled with a Christian! O my Christian ducats!
Justice! the law! my ducats, and my daughter!
A sealéd bag, two sealéd bags of ducats,
Of double ducats, stol'n from me by my daughter!
And jewels—two stones, two rich and precious stones,
Stol'n by my daughter! Justice! find the girl!
She hath the stones upon her, and the ducats!'

Salerio. Why, all the boys in Venice follow him,
Crying, his stones, his daughter, and his ducats.
Solanio. Let good Antonio look he keep his day,
Or he shall pay for this.
Salerio.   Marry, well remembred:
I reasoned with a Frenchman yesterday,
Who told me, in the narrow seas that part
The French and English, there miscarriéd
A vessel of our country richly fraught:
I thought upon Antonio when he told me,
And wished in silence that it were not his.
Solanio. You were best to tell Antonio what you hear—
Yet do not suddenly, for it may grieve him.
Salerio. A kinder gentleman treads not the earth.
I saw Bassanio and Antonio part.
Bassanio told him he would make some speed
Of his return: he answered, 'Do not so.
Slubber not business for my sake, Bassanio,
But stay the very riping of the time.
And for the Jew's bond which he hath of me,
Let it not enter in your mind of love:
Be merry, and employ your chiefest thoughts
To courtship, and such fair ostents of love
As shall conveniently become you there.'
And even there, his eye being big with tears,
Turning his face, he put his hand behind him,
And with affection wondrous sensible
He wrung Bassanio's hand, and so they parted.
Solanio. I think he only loves the world for him.
I pray thee, let us go and find him out,
And quicken his embracéd heaviness
With some delight or other.
Salerio.   Do we so.   [*they pass on*

[2.9.]   *The hall of Portia's house at Belmont*

A servitor on guard before the curtains;
NERISSA enters in haste

Nerissa. Quick, quick, I pray thee—draw the
curtain straight.
The Prince of Arragon hath ta'en his oath,
And comes to his election presently.
[*the curtains are drawn aside*

PORTIA enters with the Prince of ARRAGON,
and their trains

Portia. Behold, there stand the caskets, noble prince.
If you choose that wherein I am contained,
Straight shall our nuptial rites be solemnized:
But if you fail, without more speech, my lord,
You must be gone from hence immediately.
Arragon. I am enjoined by oath to observe
three things—
First, never to unfold to any one
Which casket 'twas I chose; next, if I fail
Of the right casket, never in my life
To woo a maid in way of marriage;
Lastly,
If I do fail in fortune of my choice,
Immediately to leave you and be gone.
Portia. To these injunctions every one doth swear,
That comes to hazard for my worthless self.
Arragon. And so have I addressed me. Fortune now
To my heart's hope!   [*he turns to look upon the caskets*
Gold, silver, and base lead....
'Who chooseth me must give and hazard all he hath.'
You shall look fairer, ere I give or hazard....

What says the golden chest? ha! let me see—
'Who chooseth me shall gain what many men desire.'
What many men desire! that 'many' may be meant
By the fool multitude, that choose by show,
Not learning more than the fond eye doth teach,
Which pries not to th'interior, but like the martlet
Builds in the weather on the outward wall,
Even in the force and road of casualty.
I will not choose what many men desire,
Because I will not jump with common spirits,
And rank me with the barbarous multitudes....
Why, then to thee, thou silver treasure-house!
Tell me once more what title thou dost bear:
'Who chooseth me shall get as much as he deserves.'
And well said too; for who shall go about
To cozen fortune and be honourable
Without the stamp of merit. Let none presume
To wear an undeservéd dignity...
O, that estates, degrees and offices,
Were not derived corruptly, and that clear honour
Were purchased by the merit of the wearer—
How many then should cover that stand bare!
How many be commanded that command!
How much low peasantry would then be gleaned
From the true seed of honour! and how much honour
Picked from the chaff and ruin of the times,
To be new varnished...Well, but to my choice....
'Who chooseth me shall get as much as he deserves.'
I will assume desert...[*he takes up the silver casket*] Give
    me a key for this—
And instantly unlock my fortunes here.
            [*he opens the casket, and starts back amazed*
  (*Portia.* Too long a pause for that which you
      find there.

Arragon. What's here? the portrait of a blinking idiot,
Presenting me a schedule! I will read it...
How much unlike art thou to Portia!
How much unlike my hopes and my deservings!
'Who chooseth me shall have as much as he deserves.'
Did I deserve no more than a fool's head?
Is that my prize? are my deserts no better?

Portia. To offend and judge are distinct offices,
And of opposéd natures.

Arragon [*unfolds the paper*].   What is here?

> 'The fire seven times tried this—
> Seven times tried that judgement is,
> That did never choose amiss.
> Some there be that shadows kiss,
> Such have but a shadow's bliss:
> There be fools alive, I wis,
> Silvered o'er—and so was this....
> Take what wife you will to bed,
> I will ever be your head:
> So be gone, you are sped.'

> Still more fool I shall appear
> By the time I linger here.
> With one fool's head I came to woo,
> But I go away with two....
> Sweet, adieu! I'll keep my oath,
> Patiently to bear my roth.

                    [*he departs with his train*

Portia. Thus hath the candle singed the moth:
O, these deliberate fools! when they do choose,
They have the wisdom by their wit to lose.

Nerissa. The ancient saying is no heresy,
Hanging and wiving goes by destiny.

Portia. Come, draw the curtain, Nerissa. [*she does so*

A servant enters

Servant. Where is my lady?

Portia.   Here—what would my lord?

Servant. Madam, there is alighted at your gate
A young Venetian, one that comes before
To signify th'approaching of his lord,
From whom he bringeth sensible regreets...
To wit, besides commends and courteous breath,
Gifts of rich value...Yet I have not seen
So likely an ambassador of love.
A day in April never came so sweet,
To show how costly summer was at hand,
As this fore-spurrer comes before his lord.

Portia. No more, I pray thee. I am half afeard,
Thou wilt say anon he is some kin to thee,
Thou spend'st such high-day wit in praising him...
Come, come, Nerissa, for I long to see
Quick Cupid's post that comes so mannerly.

Nerissa. Bassanio—Lord Love, if thy will it be! [*they go*

[3. 1.]   *The street before Shylock's house*

SOLANIO *and* SALERIO *meeting*

Solanio. Now, what news on the Rialto?

Salerio. Why, yet it lives there unchecked that
Antonio hath a ship of rich lading wracked on the
narrow seas; the Goodwins, I think they call the place—
a very dangerous flat and fatal, where the carcases of
many a tall ship lie buried, as they say, if my gossip
Report be an honest woman of her word.

Solanio. I would she were as lying a gossip in that,
as ever knapped ginger, or made her neighbours believe
she wept for the death of a third husband...But it is

true, without any slips of prolixity or crossing the plain
highway of talk, that the good Antonio, the honest
Antonio...O, that I had a title good enough to keep his
name company—

Salerio. Come, the full stop.

Solanio. Ha! what sayest thou? Why, the end is, he
hath lost a ship.

Salerio. I would it might prove the end of his losses.

Solanio. Let me say 'amen' betimes, lest the devil
cross my prayer, for here he comes in the likeness of
a Jew....

SHYLOCK comes from his house

How now, Shylock! what news among the merchants?

Shylock [*turns upon them*]. You knew, none so well,
none so well as you, of my daughter's flight.

Salerio. That's certain! I, for my part, knew the
tailor that made the wings she flew withal.

Solanio. And Shylock, for his own part, knew the
bird was fledge, and then it is the complexion of them
all to leave the dam.

Shylock. She is damned for it.

Salerio. That's certain, if the devil may be her judge.

Shylock. My own flesh and blood to rebel!

Solanio. Out upon it, old carrion, rebels it at these
years?

Shylock. I say, my daughter is my flesh and blood.

Salerio. There is more difference between thy flesh
and hers than between jet and ivory, more between
your bloods than there is between red wine and rhenish...
But tell us, do you hear whether Antonio have had any
loss at sea or no?

Shylock. There I have another bad match—a bankrupt, a prodigal, who dare scarce show his head on the

Rialto, a beggar that was used to come so smug upon the mart...let him look to his bond! he was wont to call me usurer, let him look to his bond! he was wont to lend money for a Christian curtsy, let him look to his bond!

Salerio. Why, I am sure, if he forfeit, thou wilt not take his flesh—what's that good for?

Shylock. To bait fish withal! if it will feed nothing else, it will feed my revenge...He hath disgraced me and hindred me half a million, laughed at my losses, mocked at my gains, scorned my nation, thwarted my bargains, cooled my friends, heated mine enemies—and what's his reason? I am a Jew...Hath not a Jew eyes? hath not a Jew hands, organs, dimensions, senses, affections, passions? fed with the same food, hurt with the same weapons, subject to the same diseases, healed by the same means, warmed and cooled by the same winter and summer, as a Christian is? If you prick us, do we not bleed? if you tickle us, do we not laugh? if you poison us, do we not die? and if you wrong us, shall we not revenge? if we are like you in the rest, we will resemble you in that....If a Jew wrong a Christian, what is his humility? Revenge. If a Christian wrong a Jew, what should his sufferance be by Christian example? Why, revenge. The villainy you teach me I will execute, and it shall go hard but I will better the instruction.

A servant accosts Solanio and Salerio

Servant. Gentlemen, my master Antonio is at his house, and desires to speak with you both.

Salerio. We have been up and down to seek him.

TUBAL appears making for Shylock's house

Solanio. Here comes another of the tribe—a third cannot be matched, unless the devil himself turn Jew.

[*Solanio and Salerio depart, followed by the servant*

Shylock. How now, Tubal! what news from Genoa? hast thou found my daughter?

Tubal. I often came where I did hear of her, but cannot find her.

Shylock. Why there, there, there, there—a diamond gone, cost me two thousand ducats in Frankfort—the curse never fell upon our nation till now, I never felt it till now—two thousand ducats in that, and other precious, precious jewels...I would my daughter were dead at my foot, and the jewels in her ear! would she were hearsed at my foot, and the ducats in her coffin! No news of them? Why, so—and I know not what's spent in the search: why, thou loss upon loss! the thief gone with so much and so much to find the thief, and no satisfaction, no revenge, nor no ill luck stirring but what lights o' my shoulders, no sighs but o' my breathing, no tears but o' my shedding.   [*he weeps*

Tubal. Yes, other men have ill luck too. Antonio, as I heard in Genoa—

Shylock. What, what, what? ill luck, ill luck?

Tubal. —hath an argosy cast away, coming from Tripolis.

Shylock. I thank God, I thank God! Is it true? is it true?

Tubal. I spoke with some of the sailors that escaped the wrack.

Shylock. I thank thee good Tubal, good news, good news: ha, ha! there in Genoa.

Tubal. Your daughter spent in Genoa, as I heard, one night, fourscore ducats.

Shylock. Thou stick'st a dagger in me. I shall never see my gold again—fourscore ducats at a sitting! fourscore ducats!

Tubal. There came divers of Antonio's creditors in

my company to Venice, that swear he cannot choose
but break.

Shylock. I am very glad of it, I'll plague him, I'll
torture him, I am glad of it.

Tubal. One of them showed me a ring that he had
of your daughter for a monkey.

Shylock. Out upon her! thou torturest me, Tubal—it was
my turquoise—I had it of Leah when I was a bachelor:
I would not have given it for a wilderness of monkeys.

Tubal. But Antonio is certainly undone.

Shylock. Nay, that's true, that's very true, go Tubal,
fee me an officer, bespeak him a fortnight before. I will
have the heart of him if he forfeit, for were he out of
Venice I can make what merchandise I will...Go,
Tubal, and meet me at our synagogue—go, good Tubal
—at our synagogue, Tubal.

[*Tubal departs and Shylock goes within*

[3.2.] *The hall of Portia's house at Belmont; the curtains
are drawn back from before the caskets; in the gallery
sit musicians*

BASSANIO *with* PORTIA, GRATIANO *with* NERISSA;
the servitor and other attendants

Portia. I pray you tarry, pause a day or two
Before you hazard, for in choosing wrong
I lose your company; therefore, forbear awhile.
There's something tells me (but it is not love)
I would not lose you, and you know yourself,
Hate counsels not in such a quality;
But lest you should not understand me well—
And yet a maiden hath no tongue but thought—
I would detain you here some month or two
Before you venture for me....I could teach you

How to choose right, but then I am forsworn,
So will I never be, so may you miss me,
But if you do, you'll make me wish a sin,
That I had been forsworn...Beshrew your eyes,
They have o'er-looked me and divided me,
One half of me is yours, the other half yours—
Mine own I would say: but if mine then yours,
And so all yours...O, these naughty times
Put bars between the owners and their rights,
And so though yours, not yours. Prove it so—
Let Fortune go to hell for it, not I....
I speak too long, but 'tis to peise the time,
To eke it and to draw it out in length,
To stay you from election.

 Bassanio.   Let me choose,
For as I am, I live upon the rack.

 Portia. Upon the rack, Bassanio? then confess
What treason there is mingled with your love.

 Bassanio. None but that ugly treason of mistrust,
Which makes me fear th'enjoying of my love.
There may as well be amity and life
'Tween snow and fire, as treason and my love.

 Portia. Ay, but I fear you speak upon the rack,
Where men enforcéd do speak any thing.

 Bassanio. Promise me life, and I'll confess the truth.

 Portia. Well then, confess and live.

 Bassanio.   'Confess' and 'love'
Had been the very sum of my confession:
O happy torment, when my torturer
Doth teach me answers for deliverance...
But let me to my fortune and the caskets.

 Portia. Away then! I am locked in one of them—
If you do love me, you will find me out....
Nerissa and the rest, stand all aloof.

Let music sound while he doth make his choice—
Then if he lose, he makes a swan-like end,
Fading in music....[*all but the servitor go up into the gallery*
                That the comparison
May stand more proper, my eye shall be the stream,
And wat'ry death-bed for him...He may win,
And what is music then? then music is
Even as the flourish when true subjects bow
To a new-crownéd monarch: such it is,
As are those dulcet sounds in break of day
That creep into the dreaming bridegroom's ear,
And summon him to marriage....Now he goes,
With no less presence, but with much more love,
Than young Alcides, when he did redeem
The virgin tribute paid by howling Troy
To the sea-monster: I stand for sacrifice:
The rest aloof are the Dardanian wives,
With blearéd visages, come forth to view
The issue of th'exploit...Go, Hercules!
Live thou, I live. With much much more dismay
I view the fight than thou that mak'st the fray.

   '*A song, the whilst* BASSANIO *comments on the caskets
                to himself*'

        Tell me where is Fancy bred,
        Or in the heart, or in the head?
        How begot, how nourishéd?
All. Reply, reply.

        It is engendred in the eyes,
        With gazing fed, and Fancy dies...
        In the cradle where it lies.
           Let us all ring Fancy's knell....
           I'll begin it—Ding, dong, bell.
All. Ding, dong, bell.

Bassanio. So may the outward shows be least themselves—
The world is still deceived with ornament.
In law, what plea so tainted and corrupt,
But, being seasoned with a gracious voice,
Obscures the show of evil? In religion,
What damnéd error, but some sober brow
Will bless it, and approve it with a text,
Hiding the grossness with fair ornament?
There is no vice so simple, but assumes
Some mark of virtue on his outward parts;
How many cowards, whose hearts are all as false
As stairs of sand, wear yet upon their chins
The beards of Hercules and frowning Mars,
Who, inward searched, have livers white as milk?
And these assume but valour's excrement
To render them redoubted....Look on beauty,
And you shall see 'tis purchased by the weight,
Which therein works a miracle in nature,
Making them lightest that wear most of it:
So are those crispéd snaky golden locks
Which make such wanton gambols with the wind,
Upon supposéd fairness, often known
To be the dowry of a second head,
The skull that bred them in the sepulchre....
Thus ornament is but the guiléd shore
To a most dangerous sea; the beauteous scarf
Veiling an Indian beauty; in a word,
The seeming truth which cunning times put on
To entrap the wisest....Therefore, thou gaudy gold,
Hard food for Midas, I will none of thee—
Nor none of thee, thou pale and common drudge
'Tween man and man: but thou, thou meagre lead,
Which rather threaten'st than dost promise aught,
Thy plainness moves me more than eloquence,

And here choose I—joy be the consequence!

[the servitor gives him the key

(*Portia.* How all the other passions fleet to air,
As doubtful thoughts, and rash-embraced despair,
And shudd'ring fear and green-eyed jealousy...
O love, be moderate, allay thy ecstasy,
In measure rain thy joy, scant this excess—
I feel too much thy blessing, make it less,
For fear I surfeit!

Bassanio [opens the leaden casket]. What find I here?
Fair Portia's counterfeit....What demi-god
Hath come so near creation? Move these eyes?
Or whether, riding on the balls of mine,
Seem they in motion? Here are severed lips,
Parted with sugar breath—so sweet a bar
Should sunder such sweet friends: here in her hairs
The painter plays the spider, and hath woven
A golden mesh t'entrap the hearts of men,
Faster than gnats in cobwebs—But her eyes!
How could he see to do them? having made one,
Methinks it should have power to steal both his,
And leave itself unfurnished: yet look, how far
The substance of my praise doth wrong this shadow
In underprizing it, so far this shadow
Doth limp behind the substance....Here's the scroll,
The continent and summary of my fortune.

> 'You that choose not by the view
> Chance as fair and choose as true:
> Since this fortune falls to you,
> Be content, and seek no new.
> If you be well pleased with this,
> And hold your fortune for your bliss,
> Turn you where your lady is,
> And claim her with a loving kiss.'

A gentle scroll...[*he turns to Portia*] Fair lady, by
    your leave,
I come by note, to give and to receive.
Like one of two contending in a prize,
That thinks he hath done well in people's eyes,
Hearing applause and universal shout,
Giddy in spirit, still gazing in a doubt
Whether those peals of praise be his or no,
So thrice-fair lady stand I, even so,
As doubtful whether what I see be true,
Until confirmed, signed, ratified by you.
  Portia. You see me, Lord Bassanio, where I stand,
Such as I am; though for myself alone
I would not be ambitious in my wish
To wish myself much better, yet for you
I would be trebled twenty times myself—
A thousand times more fair, ten thousand times
More rich—
That only to stand high in your account,
I might in virtues, beauties, livings, friends,
Exceed account: but the full sum of me
Is some of something...which, to term in gross,
Is an unlessoned girl, unschooled, unpractised,
Happy in this, she is not yet so old
But she may learn; happier than this,
She is not bred so dull but she can learn;
Happiest of all is that her gentle spirit
Commits itself to yours to be directed,
As from her lord, her governor, her king.... [*they kiss*
Myself and what is mine to you and yours
Is now converted....But now I was the lord
Of this fair mansion, master of my servants,
Queen o'er myself; and even now, but now,
This house, these servants, and this same myself,

Are yours—my lord's!—I give them with this ring,
Which when you part from, lose, or give away,
Let it presage the ruin of your love,
And be my vantage to exclaim on you.

Bassanio. Madam, you have bereft me of all words,
Only my blood speaks to you in my veins,
And there is such confusion in my powers,
As after some oration fairly spoke
By a belovéd prince there doth appear
Among the buzzing pleaséd multitude,
Where every something, being blent together,
Turns to a wild of nothing, save of joy,
Expressed and not expressed...But when this ring
Parts from this finger, then parts life from hence!
O, then be bold to say Bassanio's dead.

NERISSA *and* GRATIANO *descend*

Nerissa. My lord and lady, it is now our time,
That have stood by and seen our wishes prosper,
To cry 'good joy.' Good joy, my lord, and lady!

Gratiano. My Lord Bassanio, and my gentle lady,
I wish you all the joy that you can wish;
For I am sure you can wish none from me:
And, when your honours mean to solemnize
The bargain of your faith, I do beseech you,
Even at that time I may be married too.

Bassanio. With all my heart, so thou canst get a wife.

Gratiano. I thank your lordship, you have got
      me one....   [*he takes Nerissa by the hand*
My eyes, my lord, can look as swift as yours:
You saw the mistress, I beheld the maid;
You loved, I loved—for intermission
No more pertains to me, my lord, than you;
Your fortune stood upon the caskets there,

And so did mine too, as the matter falls:
For wooing here until I sweat again,
And swearing till my very roof was dry
With oaths of love, at last—if promise last—
I got a promise of this fair one here,
To have her love...provided that your fortune
Achieved her mistress.

    Portia.   Is this true, Nerissa?

    Nerissa. Madam, it is, so you stand pleased withal.

    Bassanio. And do you, Gratiano, mean good faith?

    Gratiano. Yes, faith, my lord.

    Bassanio. Our feast shall be much honoured in
       your marriage.

    Gratiano. We'll play with them the first boy for a
thousand ducats.

    Nerissa. What! and stake down?

    Gratiano. No, we shall ne'er win at that sport, and
stake down....

    LORENZO, *JESSICA, and* SALERIO *enter the chamber*

But who comes here? Lorenzo and his infidel?
What, and my old Venetian friend, Salerio?

    Bassanio. Lorenzo and Salerio, welcome hither,
If that the youth of my new interest here
Have power to bid you welcome...[*to Portia*] By
       your leave,
I bid my very friends and countrymen,
Sweet Portia, welcome.

    Portia.   So do I, my lord.
They are entirely welcome.

    Lorenzo. I thank your honour. For my part, my lord,
My purpose was not to have seen you here,
But meeting with Salerio by the way,
He did entreat me, past all saying nay,

To come with him along.

Salerio.   I did, my lord,
And I have reason for it. Signior Antonio
Commends him to you.   *[he gives Bassanio a letter*

Bassanio.   Ere I ope his letter,
I pray you, tell me how my good friend doth.

Salerio. Not sick, my lord, unless it be in mind—
Nor well, unless in mind: his letter there
Will show you his estate.   *[Bassanio opens the letter*

Gratiano. Nerissa, cheer yon stranger, bid
     her welcome....

       [Nerissa greets Jessica; Gratiano salutes Salerio
Your hand, Salerio. What's the news from Venice?
How doth that royal merchant, good Antonio? *[aside*
I know he will be glad of our success,
We are the Jasons, we have won the fleece!

Salerio. I would you had won the fleece that he
     hath lost.   *[they talk apart*

Portia. There are some shrewd contents in yon
     same paper,
That steals the colour from Bassanio's cheek—
Some dear friend dead, else nothing in the world
Could turn so much the constitution
Of any constant man...What, worse and worse!

             [she lays her hand upon his arm
With leave, Bassanio—I am half yourself,
And I must freely have the half of anything
That this same paper brings you.

Bassanio.   O sweet Portia,
Here are a few of the unpleasant'st words,
That ever blotted paper....Gentle lady,
When I did first impart my love to you,
I freely told you all the wealth I had
Ran in my veins—I was a gentleman—

And then I told you true: and yet, dear lady,
Rating myself at nothing, you shall see
How much I was a braggart. When I told you
My state was nothing, I should then have told you
That I was worse than nothing; for, indeed,
I have engaged myself to a dear friend,
Engaged my friend to his mere enemy,
To feed my means....[*with breaking voice*] Here is a
    letter, lady,
The paper as the body of my friend,
And every word in it a gaping wound,
Issuing life-blood....But is it true, Salerio?
Have all his ventures failed? What, not one hit?
From Tripolis, from Mexico, and England,
From Lisbon, Barbary, and India?
And not one vessel scape the dreadful touch
Of merchant-marring rocks?
  Salerio.   Not one, my lord.
Besides, it should appear, that if he had
The present money to discharge the Jew,
He would not take it: never did I know
A creature that did bear the shape of man
So keen and greedy to confound a man.
He plies the duke at morning and at night,
And doth impeach the freedom of the state,
If they deny him justice. Twenty merchants,
The duke himself, and the magnificoes
Of greatest port, have all persuaded with him,
But none can drive him from the envious plea
Of forfeiture, of justice, and his bond.
  Jessica. When I was with him, I have heard
    him swear
To Tubal and to Chus, his countrymen,
That he would rather have Antonio's flesh

Than twenty times the value of the sum
That he did owe him: and I know, my lord,
If law, authority, and power deny not,
It will go hard with poor Antonio.

Portia. Is it your dear friend that is thus in trouble?

Bassanio. The dearest friend to me, the kindest man,
The best-conditioned and unwearied spirit
In doing courtesies: and one in whom
The ancient Roman honour more appears
Than any that draws breath in Italy.

Portia. What sum owes he the Jew?

Bassanio. For me, three thousand ducats.

Portia.   What, no more?
Pay him six thousand, and deface the bond;
Double six thousand, and then treble that,
Before a friend of this description
Shall lose a hair thorough Bassanio's fault....
First, go with me to church, and call me wife,
And then away to Venice to your friend;
For never shall you lie by Portia's side
With an unquiet soul! You shall have gold
To pay the petty debt twenty times over.
When it is paid, bring your true friend along.
My maid Nerissa and myself meantime
Will live as maids and widows...Come, away!
For you shall hence upon your wedding-day:
Bid your friends welcome, show a merry cheer,
Since you are dear bought, I will love you dear....
But let me hear the letter of your friend.

Bassanio [*reads*]. 'Sweet Bassanio, my ships have all miscarried, my creditors grow cruel, my estate is very low, my bond to the Jew is forfeit, and since, in paying it, it is impossible I should live, all debts are cleared between you and I, if I might but see you at my death:

notwithstanding, use your pleasure—if your love do
not persuade you to come, let not my letter.'

Portia. O love, dispatch all business, and be gone!

Bassanio. Since I have your good leave to go away,
I will make haste; but, till I come again,
No bed shall e'er be guilty of my stay,
No rest be interposer 'twixt us twain.

[*they hurry forth*

[3.3.]   *The street before Shylock's house*

SHYLOCK (*at his door*), SOLANIO, ANTONIO,
and a Gaoler

Shylock. Gaoler, look to him—tell not me of mercy—
This is the fool that lent out money gratis.
Gaoler, look to him.

Antonio.   Hear me yet, good Shylock.

Shylock. I'll have my bond, speak not against my bond,
I have sworn an oath that I will have my bond:
Thou call'dst me dog before thou hadst a cause,
But since I am a dog beware my fangs.
The duke shall grant me justice. I do wonder,
Thou naughty gaoler, that thou art so fond
To come abroad with him at his request.

Antonio. I pray thee, hear me speak.

Shylock. I'll have my bond—I will not hear
    thee speak.
I'll have my bond, and therefore speak no more.
I'll not be made a soft and dull-eyed fool,
To shake the head, relent, and sigh, and yield
To Christian intercessors...Follow not—
I'll have no speaking, I will have my bond.

        [*he goes within, slamming the door behind him*

Solanio. It is the most impenetrable cur,
That ever kept with men.

Antonio. Let him alone,
I'll follow him no more with bootless prayers.
He seeks my life—his reason well I know;
I oft delivered from his forfeitures
Many that have at times made moan to me.
Therefore he hates me.

Solanio. I am sure, the duke
Will never grant this forfeiture to hold.

Antonio. The duke cannot deny the course of law:
For the commodity that strangers have
With us in Venice, if it be denied,
Will much impeach the justice of the state,
Since that the trade and profit of the city
Consisteth of all nations....Therefore, go.
These griefs and losses have so bated me,
That I shall hardly spare a pound of flesh
To-morrow to my bloody creditor....
Well, gaoler, on. Pray God, Bassanio come
To see me pay his debt, and then I care not! *[they go*

[3.4.] *The hall of Portia's house at Belmont*

PORTIA, NERISSA, LORENZO, *JESSICA, and a man
of Portia's, called* BALTHAZAR

Lorenzo. Madam, although I speak it in your presence,
You have a noble and a true conceit
Of god-like amity, which appears most strongly
In bearing thus the absence of your lord.
But if you knew to whom you show this honour,
How true a gentleman you send relief,
How dear a lover of my lord your husband,

I know you would be prouder of the work,
Than customary bounty can enforce you.
  Portia. I never did repent for doing good,
Nor shall not now: for in companions
That do converse and waste the time together,
Whose souls do bear an egall yoke of love,
There must be needs a like proportion
Of lineaments, of manners, and of spirit;
Which makes me think that this Antonio,
Being the bosom lover of my lord,
Must needs be like my lord. If it be so,
How little is the cost I have bestowed
In purchasing the semblance of my soul
From out the state of hellish cruelty?
This comes too near the praising of myself,
Therefore no more of it: hear other things.
Lorenzo, I commit into your hands
The husbandry and manage of my house,
Until my lord's return: for mine own part,
I have toward heaven breathed a secret vow
To live in prayer and contemplation,
Only attended by Nerissa here,
Until her husband and my lord's return.
There is a monastery two miles off,
And there we will abide....I do desire you
Not to deny this imposition,
The which my love and some necessity
Now lays upon you.
  Lorenzo [*bows*].   Madam, with all my heart—
I shall obey you in all fair commands.
  Portia. My people do already know my mind,
And will acknowledge you and Jessica
In place of Lord Bassanio and myself....
So fare you well, till we shall meet again.
  Lorenzo. Fair thoughts and happy hours attend on you!

Jessica. I wish your ladyship all heart's content.
Portia. I thank you for your wish, and am
    well pleased
To wish it back on you: fare you well, Jessica....
                    [*Jessica and Lorenzo go out*
Now, Balthazar,
As I have ever found thee honest-true,
So let me find thee still...Take this same letter,
And use thou all th'endeavour of a man
In speed to Padua, see thou render this
Into my cousin's hand, Doctor Bellario,
And, look, what notes and garments he doth give thee,
Bring them, I pray thee, with imagined speed
†Unto the tranect, to the common ferry
Which trades to Venice...Waste no time in words,
But get thee gone. I shall be there before thee.
    Balthazar. Madam, I go with all convenient speed.
                        [*he departs*
    Portia. Come on, Nerissa—I have work in hand
That you yet know not of; we'll see our husbands
Before they think of us!
    Nerissa.   Shall they see us?
    Portia. They shall, Nerissa; but in such a habit,
That they shall think we are accomplishéd
With what we lack...I'll hold thee any wager,
When we are both accoutred like young men,
I'll prove the prettier fellow of the two,
And wear my dagger with the braver grace,
And speak between the change of man and boy
With a reed-voice, and turn two mincing steps
Into a manly stride; and speak of frays
Like a fine bragging youth; and tell quaint lies,
How honourable ladies sought my love,
Which I denying, they fell sick and died—
I could not do withal! Then I'll repent,

And wish, for all that, that I had not killed them;
And twenty of these puny lies I'll tell,
That men shall swear I have discontinued school
Above a twelvemonth...I have within my mind
A thousand raw tricks of these bragging Jacks,
Which I will practise.

   Nerissa.   Why, shall we turn to men?

   Portia. Fie, what a question's that,
If thou wert near a lewd interpreter...
But come, I'll tell thee all my whole device,
When I am in my coach, which stays for us
At the park-gate; and therefore haste away,
For we must measure twenty miles to-day.

                          [they hurry forth

[3.5.] *An avenue of trees leading up to Portia's house;
on either side, grassy banks and lawns set with cypresses*

   LANCELOT and JESSICA approach in conversation

Lancelot. Yes truly, for look you, the sins of the
father are to be laid upon the children—therefore, I
promise you, I fear you. I was always plain with you,
and so now I speak my agitation of the matter: therefore,
be o' good cheer, for truly I think you are damned. There
is but one hope in it that can do you any good, and that
is but a kind of bastard hope neither.

   Jessica. And what hope is that, I pray thee?

   Lancelot. Marry, you may partly hope that your
father got you not, that you are not the Jew's daughter.

   Jessica. That were a kind of bastard hope, indeed!
So the sins of my mother should be visited upon me.

   Lancelot. Truly then I fear you are damned both by
father and mother: thus when I shun Scylla, your

father, I fall into Charybdis, your mother: well, you are gone both ways.

Jessica. I shall be saved by my husband—he hath made me a Christian.

Lancelot. Truly, the more to blame he. We were Christians enow before, e'en as many as could well live, one by another...This making of Christians will raise the price of hogs—if we grow all to be pork-eaters, we shall not shortly have a rasher on the coals for money.

LORENZO *is seen coming from the house*

Jessica. I'll tell my husband, Lancelot, what you say—here he comes.

Lorenzo. I shall grow jealous of you shortly, Lancelot, if you thus get my wife into corners.

Jessica. Nay, you need not fear us, Lorenzo. Lancelot and I are out. He tells me flatly there's no mercy for me in heaven, because I am a Jew's daughter: and he says you are no good member of the commonwealth, for, in converting Jews to Christians, you raise the price of pork.

Lorenzo. I shall answer that better to the commonwealth than you can the getting up of the negro's belly: the Moor is with child by you, Lancelot.

Lancelot. It is much that the Moor should be more than reason: but if she be less than an honest woman, she is indeed more than I took her for.

Lorenzo. How every fool can play upon the word! I think the best grace of wit will shortly turn into silence, and discourse grow commendable in none only but parrots...Go in, sirrah—bid them prepare for dinner.

Lancelot. That is done, sir—they have all stomachs.

Lorenzo. Goodly Lord, what a wit-snapper are you! then bid them prepare dinner.

Lancelot. That is done too, sir—only 'cover' is the word.

Lorenzo. Will you cover then, sir?

Lancelot. Not so, sir, neither—I know my duty.

Lorenzo. Yet more quarrelling with occasion! Wilt thou show the whole wealth of thy wit in an instant? I pray thee, understand a plain man in his plain meaning: go to thy fellows, bid them cover the table, serve in the meat, and we will come in to dinner.

Lancelot. For the table, sir, it shall be served in— for the meat, sir, it shall be covered—for your coming in to dinner, sir, why, let it be as humours and conceits shall govern. *[he goes within*

Lorenzo. O dear discretion, how his words are suited! The fool hath planted in his memory
An army of good words, and I do know
A many fools that stand in better place
Garnished like him, that for a tricksy word
Defy the matter...How cheer'st thou, Jessica?
And now, good sweet, say thy opinion,
How dost thou like the Lord Bassanio's wife?

Jessica. Past all expressing. It is very meet,
The Lord Bassanio live an upright life,
For having such a blessing in his lady
He finds the joys of heaven here on earth,
†And if on earth he do not merit it,
In reason he should never come to heaven!
Why, if two gods should play some heavenly match,
And on the wager lay two earthly women,
And Portia one, there must be something else
Pawned with the other, for the poor rude world
Hath not her fellow.

Lorenzo. Even such a husband
Hast thou of me, as she is for a wife.

Jessica. Nay, but ask my opinion too of that.

Lorenzo. I will anon—first, let us go to dinner.

Jessica. Nay, let me praise you while I have
    a stomach.

Lorenzo. No, pray thee, let it serve for table-talk—
Then, howsome'er thou speak'st, 'mong other things
I shall digest it.

Jessica.   Well, I'll set you forth.

                  [they go in to dinner

[4. 1.]   *A Court of Justice; on a platform at the back
a great chair of state with three lower chairs on either
side; before these a table for clerks, lawyers' desks, etc.*

ANTONIO (*guarded*), BASSANIO, GRATIANO, SOLANIO,
officers, clerks, attendants, and a concourse of people. The
DUKE *in white and six Magnificoes in red enter in state
and take their seats*

Duke. What, is Antonio here?

Antonio. Ready, so please your grace.

Duke. I am sorry for thee—thou art come to answer
A stony adversary, an inhuman wretch
Uncapable of pity, void and empty
From any dram of mercy.

Antonio.   I have heard,
Your grace hath ta'en great pains to qualify
His rigorous course; but since he stands obdurate,
And that no lawful means can carry me
Out of his envy's reach, I do oppose
My patience to his fury, and am armed
To suffer with a quietness of spirit
The very tyranny and rage of his.

Duke. Go one, and call the Jew into the court.

Solanio. He is ready at the door, he comes, my lord.

Duke. Make room, and let him stand before
our face....

The crowd parts, and SHYLOCK *confronts the Duke;
he bows low*

Shylock, the world thinks, and I think so too,
That thou but leadest this fashion of thy malice
To the last hour of act, and then 'tis thought
Thou'lt show thy mercy and remorse more strange
Than is thy strange apparent cruelty;
And where thou now exacts the penalty,
Which is a pound of this poor merchant's flesh,
Thou wilt not only loose the forfeiture,
But touched with human gentleness and love,
Forgive a moiety of the principal;
Glancing an eye of pity on his losses,
That have of late so huddled on his back;
Enow to press a royal merchant down,
And pluck commiseration of his state
From brassy bosoms and rough hearts of flint,
From stubborn Turks and Tartars, never trained
To offices of tender courtesy...
We all expect a gentle answer, Jew.
    Shylock. I have possessed your grace of what I purpose,
And by our holy Sabbath have I sworn
To have the due and forfeit of my bond.
If you deny it, let the danger light
Upon your charter and your city's freedom!
You'll ask me why I rather choose to have
A weight of carrion flesh than to receive
Three thousand ducats: I'll not answer that!
But say it is my humour, is it answered?
What if my house be troubled with a rat,
And I be pleased to give ten thousand ducats

To have it baned? what, are you answered yet?
Some men there are love not a gaping pig,
Some that are mad if they behold a cat,
And others when the bag-pipe sings i'th' nose
Cannot contain their urine: for affection,
Master of passion, sways it to the mood
Of what it likes or loathes. Now, for your answer:
As there is no firm reason to be rendred,
Why he cannot abide a gaping pig;
Why he, a harmless necessary cat;
Why he, a woollen bag-pipe; but of force
Must yield to such inevitable shame,
As to offend, himself being offended;
So can I give no reason, nor I will not,
More than a lodged hate and a certain loathing
I bear Antonio, that I follow thus
A losing suit against him! Are you answered?
  Bassanio. This is no answer, thou unfeeling man,
To excuse the current of thy cruelty!
  Shylock. I am not bound to please thee with
      my answers!
  Bassanio. Do all men kill the things they do not love?
  Shylock. Hates any man the thing he would not kill?
  Bassanio. Every offence is not a hate at first!
  Shylock. What, wouldst thou have a serpent sting
      thee twice?
  Antonio. I pray you, think you question with the Jew.
You may as well go stand upon the beach
And bid the main flood bate his usual height,
You may as well use question with the wolf
Why he hath made the ewe bleat for the lamb;
You may as well forbid the mountain pines
To wag their high tops and to make no noise,
When they are fretten with the gusts of heaven;

You may as well do any thing most hard,
As seek to soften that—than which what's harder?—
His Jewish heart! Therefore, I do beseech you,
Make no mo offers, use no farther means,
But with all brief and plain conveniency
Let me have judgement and the Jew his will!
  Bassanio. For thy three thousand ducats here is six.
  Shylock. If every ducat in six thousand ducats
Were in six parts and every part a ducat,
I would not draw them, I would have my bond!
  Duke. How shalt thou hope for mercy, rendring none?
  Shylock. What judgement shall I dread, doing
      no wrong?
You have among you many a purchased slave,
Which, like your asses and your dogs and mules,
You use in abject and in slavish parts,
Because you bought them—shall I say to you,
Let them be free, marry them to your heirs?
Why sweat they under burthens? let their beds
Be made as soft as yours, and let their palates
Be seasoned with such viands? You will answer,
'The slaves are ours.' So do I answer you...
The pound of flesh, which I demand of him,
Is dearly bought, 'tis mine, and I will have it:
If you deny me, fie upon your law!
There is no force in the decrees of Venice...
I stand for judgement. Answer—shall I have it?
  Duke. Upon my power, I may dismiss this court,
Unless Bellario, a learned doctor,
Whom I have sent for to determine this,
Come here to-day.
  Solanio.   My lord, here stays without
A messenger with letters from the doctor,
New come from Padua.

Duke. Bring us the letters; call the messenger.

Bassanio. Good cheer, Antonio! what man, courage yet:
The Jew shall have my flesh, blood, bones, and all,
Ere thou shalt lose for me one drop of blood.

[*Shylock takes a knife from his girdle and kneels to whet it*

Antonio. I am a tainted wether of the flock,
Meetest for death. The weakest kind of fruit
Drops earliest to the ground, and so let me;
You cannot better be employed, Bassanio,
Than to live still, and write mine epitaph.

NERISSA enters, dressed as a lawyer's clerk

Duke. Came you from Padua, from Bellario?

Nerissa [*bows*]. From both, my lord. Bellario greets
your grace.

[*she presents a letter; the Duke opens and reads it*

Bassanio. Why dost thou whet thy knife so earnestly?

Shylock. To cut the forfeiture from that bankrupt there.

Gratiano. Not on thy sole, but on thy soul, harsh Jew,
Thou mak'st thy knife keen: but no metal can,
No, not the hangman's axe, bear half the keenness
Of thy sharp envy: can no prayers pierce thee?

Shylock. No, none that thou hast wit enough to make.

Gratiano. O, be thou damned, inexorable dog,
And for thy life let justice be accused!
Thou almost mak'st me waver in my faith,
To hold opinion with Pythagoras
That souls of animals infuse themselves
Into the trunks of men: thy currish spirit
Governed a Wolf, who hanged for human slaughter,
Even from the gallows did his fell soul fleet,
And whilst thou layest in thy unhallowed dam,
Infused itself in thee; for thy desires
Are wolvish, bloody, starved, and ravenous.

Shylock. Till thou canst rail the seal from off my bond,
Thou but offend'st thy lungs to speak so loud:
Repair thy wit, good youth, or it will fall
To cureless ruin....I stand here for law.

Duke. This letter from Bellario doth commend
A young and learned doctor to our court:
Where is he?

Nerissa.   He attendeth here hard by
To know your answer, whether you'll admit him.

Duke. With all my heart: some three or four of you,
Go give him courteous conduct to this place.

                              [*attendants bow and depart*
Meantime, the court shall hear Bellario's letter....

                He reads out the letter

'Your grace shall understand that at the receipt of your
letter I am very sick, but in the instant that your messenger came, in loving visitation was with me a young doctor
of Rome, his name is Balthazar: I acquainted him with
the cause in controversy between the Jew and Antonio
the merchant, we turned o'er many books together, he
is furnished with my opinion, which bettered with his
own learning, the greatness whereof I cannot enough
commend, comes with him at my importunity to fill up
your grace's request in my stead. I beseech you, let his
lack of years be no impediment to let him lack a reverend
estimation, for I never knew so young a body with so
old a head: I leave him to your gracious acceptance,
whose trial shall better publish his commendation.'
You hear the learned Bellario, what he writes.

        PORTIA enters, dressed as a doctor of civil law,
                with a book in her hand

And here, I take it, is the doctor come....
Give me your hand. Come you from old Bellario?

Portia. I did, my lord.

Duke. You are welcome. Take your place...
    [*an attendant ushers Portia to a desk near the Duke*
Are you acquainted with the difference
That holds this present question in the court?

Portia. I am informéd throughly of the cause.
Which is the merchant here, and which the Jew?

Duke. Antonio and old Shylock, both stand forth.
                [*they step forward and bow to the Duke*
Portia. Is your name Shylock?

Shylock.   Shylock is my name.

Portia. Of a strange nature is the suit you follow,
Yet in such rule that the Venetian law
Cannot impugn you as you do proceed....
You stand within his danger, do you not?

Antonio. Ay, so he says.

Portia.   Do you confess the bond?

Antonio. I do.

Portia.   Then must the Jew be merciful.

Shylock. On what compulsion must I? tell me that.

Portia. The quality of mercy is not strained,
It droppeth as the gentle rain from heaven
Upon the place beneath: it is twice blessed;
It blesseth him that gives, and him that takes,
'Tis mightiest in the mightiest, it becomes
The thronéd monarch better than his crown,
His sceptre shows the force of temporal power,
The attribute to awe and majesty,
Wherein doth sit the dread and fear of kings:
But mercy is above this sceptred sway,
It is enthronéd in the hearts of kings,
It is an attribute to God himself;
And earthly power doth then show likest God's,
When mercy seasons justice: therefore, Jew,

Though justice be thy plea, consider this,
That in the course of justice none of us
Should see salvation: we do pray for mercy,
And that same prayer doth teach us all to render
The deeds of mercy....I have spoke thus much,
To mitigate the justice of thy plea,
Which if thou follow, this strict court of Venice
Must needs give sentence 'gainst the merchant there.

   Shylock. My deeds upon my head! I crave the law,
The penalty and forfeit of my bond.

   Portia. Is he not able to discharge the money?

   Bassanio. Yes, here I tender it for him in the court,
Yea, twice the sum. If that will not suffice,
I will be bound to pay it ten times o'er,
On forfeit of my hands, my head, my heart.
If this will not suffice, it must appear
That malice bears down truth....[*he kneels with hands
        uplifted*] And I beseech you,
Wrest once the law to your authority—
To do a great right, do a little wrong,
And curb this cruel devil of his will.

   Portia. It must not be, there is no power in Venice
Can alter a decree establishéd:
'Twill be recorded for a precedent,
And many an error by the same example
Will rush into the state. It cannot be.

   Shylock. A Daniel come to judgement: yea,
      a Daniel!   [*he kisses the hem of her robe*
O wise young judge, how I do honour thee!

   Portia. I pray you, let me look upon the bond.

   Shylock [*swiftly snatching a paper from his bosom*]. Here
'tis, most reverend doctor, here it is.

   Portia [*taking the paper*]. Shylock, there's thrice thy
   money offered thee.

Shylock. An oath, an oath, I have an oath in heaven.
Shall I lay perjury upon my soul?
No, not for Venice.
   Portia [*perusing the paper*]. Why, this bond is forfeit,
And lawfully by this the Jew may claim
A pound of flesh, to be by him cut off
Nearest the merchant's heart...Be merciful,
Take thrice thy money, bid me tear the bond.
   Shylock. When it is paid according to the tenour....
It doth appear you are a worthy judge,
You know the law, your exposition
Hath been most sound: I charge you by the law,
Whereof you are a well-deserving pillar,
Proceed to judgement: by my soul I swear,
There is no power in the tongue of man
To alter me. I stay here on my bond.
   Antonio. Most heartily I do beseech the court
To give the judgement.
   Portia.   Why then, thus it is.
You must prepare your bosom for his knife.
   Shylock. O noble judge! O excellent young man!
   Portia. For the intent and purpose of the law
Hath full relation to the penalty,
Which here appeareth due upon the bond.
   Shylock. 'Tis very true: O wise and upright judge!
How much more elder art thou than thy looks!
   Portia. Therefore, lay bare your bosom.
   Shylock.   Ay, his breast,
So says the bond, doth it not, noble judge?
'Nearest his heart,' those are the very words.
   Portia. It is so. Are there balance here, to weigh
The flesh?
   Shylock.   I have them ready.
                    [*he opens his cloak and takes them out*

Portia. Have by some surgeon, Shylock, on your charge,
To stop his wounds, lest he do bleed to death.
Shylock. Is it so nominated in the bond?

                [he takes it and examines it closely

Portia. It is not so expressed, but what of that?
'Twere good you do so much for charity.
Shylock. I cannot find it, 'tis not in the bond.

                  [he gives it back to Portia

Portia. You merchant, have you any thing to say?
Antonio. But little; I am armed and well prepared.
Give me your hand, Bassanio, fare you well!
Grieve not that I am fall'n to this for you;
For herein Fortune shows herself more kind
Than is her custom: it is still her use,
To let the wretched man outlive his wealth,
To view with hollow eye and wrinkled brow
An age of poverty; from which ling'ring penance
Of such misery doth she cut me off....   *[they embrace*
Commend me to your honourable wife,
Tell her the process of Antonio's end,
Say how I loved you, speak me fair in death;
And when the tale is told, bid her be judge
Whether Bassanio had not once a love...
Repent but you that you shall lose your friend,
And he repents not, that he pays your debt....
For if the Jew do cut but deep enough,
I'll pay it instantly with all my heart.
Bassanio. Antonio, I am married to a wife
Which is as dear to me as life itself,
But life itself, my wife, and all the world,
Are not with me esteemed above thy life.
I would lose all, ay, sacrifice them all
Here to this devil, to deliver you.
  Portia. Your wife would give you little thanks
    for that,

If she were by, to hear you make the offer.
 Gratiano. I have a wife, whom, I protest, I love—
I would she were in heaven, so she could
Entreat some power to change this currish Jew.
 Nerissa. 'Tis well you offer it behind her back,
The wish would make else an unquiet house.
 (*Shylock.* These be the Christian husbands! I have
  a daughter—
Would any of the stock of Bárrabas
Had been her husband, rather than a Christian....
[*aloud*] We trifle time, I pray thee pursue sentence.
 Portia. A pound of that same merchant's flesh
  is thine,
The court awards it, and the law doth give it.
 Shylock. Most rightful judge!
 Portia. And you must cut this flesh from off
  his breast,
The law allows it, and the court awards it.
 Shylock. Most learnéd judge—a sentence—
  come, prepare.   [*he advances with knife drawn*
 Portia. Tarry a little, there is something else.
This bond doth give thee here no jot of blood—
The words expressly are 'a pound of flesh':
Take then thy bond, take thou thy pound of flesh,
But, in the cutting it, if thou dost shed
One drop of Christian blood, thy lands and goods
Are by the laws of Venice confiscate
Unto the state of Venice.
 Gratiano. O upright judge!—mark, Jew—O
  learnéd judge!
 Shylock. Is that the law?
 Portia [*opens her book*]. Thyself shalt see
  the act:
For, as thou urgest justice, be assured
Thou shalt have justice more than thou desir'st.

Gratiano. O learnéd judge!—mark, Jew—a
    learnéd judge!
Shylock. I take this offer then—pay the bond thrice,
And let the Christian go.
  Bassanio.   Here is the money.
  Portia.   Soft!
The Jew shall have all justice—soft, no haste—
He shall have nothing but the penalty.
  Gratiano. O Jew! an upright judge, a learnéd judge!
  Portia. Therefore, prepare thee to cut off
    the flesh.
Shed thou no blood, nor cut thou less nor more
But just a pound of flesh: if thou tak'st more
Or less than a just pound, be it but so much
As makes it light or heavy in the substance,
Or the division of the twentieth part
Of one poor scruple, nay, if the scale do turn
But in the estimation of a hair,
Thou diest and all thy goods are confiscate.
  Gratiano. A second Daniel, a Daniel, Jew!
Now, infidel, I have you on the hip.
  Portia. Why doth the Jew pause? take thy forfeiture.
  Shylock. Give me my principal, and let me go.
  Bassanio. I have it ready for thee, here it is.
  Portia. He hath refused it in the open court,
He shall have merely justice and his bond.
  Gratiano. A Daniel, still say I, a second Daniel!
I thank thee, Jew, for teaching me that word.
  Shylock. Shall I not have barely my principal?
  Portia. Thou shalt have nothing but the forfeiture
To be so taken at thy peril, Jew.
  Shylock. Why then the devil give him good of it!
I'll stay no longer question.   [*he turns to go*
  Portia.   Tarry, Jew.

The law hath yet another hold on you....

[she reads from her book

It is enacted in the laws of Venice,
If it be proved against an alien,
That by direct or indirect attempts
He seek the life of any citizen,
The party 'gainst the which he doth contrive
Shall seize one half his goods, the other half
Comes to the privy coffer of the state,
And the offender's life lies in the mercy
Of the duke only, 'gainst all other voice....

[she closes the book

In which predicament, I say, thou stand'st:
For it appears by manifest proceeding,
That indirectly and directly too
Thou hast contrived against the very life
Of the defendant; and thou hast incurred
The danger formerly by me rehearsed....
Down, therefore, and beg mercy of the duke.

  Gratiano. Beg that thou mayst have leave to
     hang thyself,
And yet thy wealth being forfeit to the state,
Thou hast not left the value of a cord,
Therefore thou must be hanged at the state's charge.

  Duke. That thou shalt see the difference of our spirit,
I pardon thee thy life before thou ask it:
For half thy wealth, it is Antonio's—
The other half comes to the general state,
Which humbleness may drive unto a fine.

  Portia. Ay, for the state, not for Antonio.

  Shylock. Nay, take my life and all, pardon not that.
You take my house, when you do take the prop
That doth sustain my house; you take my life,
When you do take the means whereby I live.

Portia. What mercy can you render him, Antonio?

Gratiano. A halter gratis—nothing else, for God's sake.

Antonio. So please my lord the duke and all
    the court
To quit the fine for one half of his goods,
I am content; so he will let me have
The other half in use, to render it
Upon his death unto the gentleman
That lately stole his daughter....
Two things provided more, that, for this favour,
He presently become a Christian;
The other, that he do record a gift,
Here in the court, of all he dies possessed,
Unto his son Lorenzo and his daughter.

Duke. He shall do this, or else I do recant
The pardon that I late pronouncéd here.

Portia. Art thou contented, Jew? what dost
    thou say?

Shylock. I am content.

Portia [*to Nerissa*].   Clerk, draw a deed of gift.

Shylock. I pray you give me leave to go from hence,
I am not well, send the deed after me,
And I will sign it.

Duke.   Get thee gone, but do it.

Gratiano. In christ'ning thou shalt have two
    godfathers—
Had I been judge, thou shouldst have had ten more,
To bring thee to the gallows, not the font.

        [*Shylock totters out amid cries of execration*

Duke [*rising*]. Sir, I entreat you home with me
    to dinner.

Portia. I humbly do desire your grace of pardon,
I must away this night toward Padua,
And it is meet I presently set forth.

Duke. I am sorry that your leisure serves you not....
                                   [*he comes down from his throne*
Antonio, gratify this gentleman,
For in my mind you are much bound to him.
                            [*the Duke, the Magnificoes and their*
                                 train depart; the crowd disperses

Bassanio. Most worthy gentleman, I and my friend
Have by your wisdom been this day acquitted
Of grievous penalties, in lieu whereof,
Three thousand ducats, due unto the Jew,
We freely cope your courteous pains withal.

Antonio. And stand indebted, over and above,
In love and service to you evermore.

Portia. He is well paid that is well satisfied,
And I, delivering you, am satisfied,
And therein do account myself well paid.
My mind was never yet more mercenary....
                              [*passing them with a bow*
I pray you, know me when we meet again.
I wish you well, and so I take my leave.

Bassanio [*hasting after*]. Dear sir, of force I must
    attempt you further.
Take some remembrance of us, as a tribute,
Not as a fee: grant me two things, I pray you,
Not to deny me, and to pardon me.

Portia [*stops at the door*]. You press me far, and
    therefore I will yield.
Give me your gloves, I'll wear them for your sake.
                                   [*he doffs them*
And, for your love, I'll take this ring from you—
Do not draw back your hand—I'll take no more,
And you in love shall not deny me this?

Bassanio. This ring, good sir—alas, it is a trifle—
I will not shame myself to give you this.

Portia. I will have nothing else but only this,
And now, methinks, I have a mind to it.
  Bassanio. There's more depends on this than on
    the value.
The dearest ring in Venice will I give you,
And find it out by proclamation,
Only for this, I pray you, pardon me.
  Portia. I see, sir, you are liberal in offers.
You taught me first to beg, and now, methinks,
You teach me how a beggar should be answered.
  Bassanio. Good sir, this ring was given me by my wife,
And when she put it on, she made me vow
That I should neither sell nor give nor lose it.
  Portia. That 'scuse serves many men to save
    their gifts.
And if your wife be not a mad-woman,
And know how well I have deserved this ring,
She would not hold out enemy for ever,
For giving it to me...Well, peace be with you!
                    [*she sweeps out, Nerissa following*
  Antonio. My Lord Bassanio, let him have the ring.
Let his deservings and my love withal
Be valued 'gainst your wife's commandment.
  Bassanio. Go, Gratiano, run and overtake him,
Give him the ring, and bring him if thou canst
Unto Antonio's house—away, make haste.
                    [*Gratiano hurries forth*
Come, you and I will thither presently,
And in the morning early will we both
Fly toward Belmont. Come, Antonio.   [*they go*

[4.2.] *A street in Venice before the Court of Justice*

PORTIA *and* NERISSA *come from the Court*

Portia [*gives a paper*]. Inquire the Jew's house out,
    give him this deed,
And let him sign it. We'll away to-night,
And be a day before our husbands home:
This deed will be well welcome to Lorenzo.

GRATIANO *comes running from the Court*

Gratiano. Fair sir, you are well o'erta'en:
My Lord Bassanio, upon more advice,
Hath sent you here this ring, and doth entreat
Your company at dinner.
Portia.   That cannot be:
His ring I do accept most thankfully,
And so I pray you tell him: furthermore,
I pray you, show my youth old Shylock's house.
Gratiano. That will I do.
Nerissa.   Sir, I would speak with you...
                            [*takes Portia aside*
I'll see if I can get my husband's ring,
Which I did make him swear to keep for ever.
Portia. Thou mayst, I warrant. We shall have
    old swearing
That they did give the rings away to men;
But we'll outface them, and outswear them too...
Away, make haste, thou know'st where I will tarry.
Nerissa [*turns to Gratiano*]. Come, good sir, will you
    show me to this house?   [*they go their ways*

[5.1.] *The avenue before Portia's house at Belmont;*
    a summer night; a moon with drifting clouds

LORENZO *and* JESSICA *pace softly beneath the trees*

Lorenzo. The moon shines bright....In such a night
    as this,
When the sweet wind did gently kiss the trees,
And they did make no noise, in such a night
Troilus methinks mounted the Troyan walls,
And sighed his soul toward the Grecian tents,
Where Cressid lay that night.

Jessica.   In such a night
Did Thisbe fearfully o'ertrip the dew,
And saw the lion's shadow ere himself,
And ran dismayed away.

Lorenzo.   In such a night
Stood Dido with a willow in her hand
Upon the wild sea banks, and waft her love
To come again to Carthage.

Jessica.   In such a night
Medea gathered the enchanted herbs
That did renew old Æson.

Lorenzo.   In such a night
Did Jessica steal from the wealthy Jew,
And with an unthrift love did run from Venice
As far as Belmont.

Jessica.   In such a night
Did young Lorenzo swear he loved her well,
Stealing her soul with many vows of faith,
And ne'er a true one.

Lorenzo.   In such a night
Did pretty Jessica (like a little shrew!)
Slander her love, and he forgave it her.

Jessica. I would out-night you, did no body come:
But, hark, I hear the footing of a man.

STEPHANO *approaches, running*

Lorenzo. Who comes so fast in silence of the night?
Stephano. A friend.
Lorenzo. A friend! what friend? your name, I pray
    you, friend?
Stephano. Stephano is my name, and I bring word
My mistress will before the break of day
Be here at Belmont—she doth stray about
By holy crosses, where she kneels and prays
For happy wedlock hours.
Lorenzo.   Who comes with her?
Stephano. None, but a holy hermit and her maid...
I pray you, is my master yet returned?
Lorenzo. He is not, nor we have not heard from him.
But go we in, I pray thee, Jessica,
And ceremoniously let us prepare
Some welcome for the mistress of the house.

LANCELOT'S *voice heard hollaing at a distance*

Lancelot. Sola, sola...wo ha, ho, sola, sola!
Lorenzo. Who calls?
Lancelot [*running in and out of the trees*]. Sola!
did you see Master Lorenzo? Master Lorenzo? sola,
sola!
Lorenzo. Leave hollaing, man—here!
Lancelot. Sola! where? where?
Lorenzo. Here!
Lancelot. Tell him, there's a post come from my
master, with his horn full of good news. My master
will be here ere morning.   [*he runs off*

Lorenzo. Sweet soul, let's in, and there expect
    their coming.
And yet no matter: why should we go in?
My friend Stephano, signify, I pray you,
Within the house, your mistress is at hand,
And bring your music forth into the air....

                                   [*Stephano goes within*

How sweet the moonlight sleeps upon this bank!
Here will we sit, and let the sounds of music
Creep in our ears—soft stillness and the night
Become the touches of sweet harmony...   [*he sits*
Sit, Jessica. Look how the floor of heaven
Is thick inlaid with patens of bright gold,
There's not the smallest orb which thou behold'st
But in his motion like an angel sings,
Still quiring to the young-eyed cherubins;
Such harmony is in immortal souls!
But whilst this muddy vesture of decay
Doth grossly close it in, we cannot hear it....

*Musicians steal from the house and bestow themselves
among the trees; they leave the door open behind them,
and a light shines therefrom*

Come, ho, and wake Diana with a hymn!
With sweetest touches pierce your mistress' ear,
And draw her home with music.   [*music*
  Jessica. I am never merry when I hear
    sweet music.
  Lorenzo. The reason is, your spirits are attentive:
For do but note a wild and wanton herd,
Or race of youthful and unhandled colts,
Fetching mad bounds, bellowing and neighing loud—
Which is the hot condition of their blood—
If they but hear perchance a trumpet sound,

Or any air of music touch their ears,
You shall perceive them make a mutual stand,
Their savage eyes turned to a modest gaze
By the sweet power of music: therefore, the poet
Did feign that Orpheus drew trees, stones, and floods,
Since nought so stockish, hard, and full of rage,
But music for the time doth change his nature.
The man that hath no music in himself,
Nor is not moved with concord of sweet sounds,
Is fit for treasons, stratagems, and spoils,
The motions of his spirit are dull as night,
And his affections dark as Erebus:
Let no such man be trusted....Mark the music.

Portia and Nerissa come slowly along the avenue

Portia. That light we see is burning in my hall...
How far that little candle throws his beams!
So shines a good deed in a naughty world.
  Nerissa. When the moon shone, we did not see
    the candle.
  Portia. So doth the greater glory dim the less—
A substitute shines brightly as a king,
Until a king be by, and then his state
Empties itself, as doth an inland brook
Into the main of waters...Music! hark!
  Nerissa. It is your music, madam, of the house.
  Portia. Nothing is good, I see, without respect—
Methinks it sounds much sweeter than by day.
  Nerissa. Silence bestows that virtue on it, madam.
  Portia. The crow doth sing as sweetly as the lark
When neither is attended: and I think
The nightingale, if she should sing by day
When every goose is cackling, would be thought
No better a musician than the wren.

How many things by season seasoned are
To their right praise and true perfection...
Peace, ho! the moon sleeps with Endymion,
And would not be awaked.   [*the music ceases*
    Lorenzo.   That is the voice,
Or I am much deceived, of Portia.
    Portia. He knows me, as the blind man knows
        the cuckoo,
By the bad voice.
    Lorenzo.   Dear lady, welcome home.
    Portia. We have been praying for our husbands'
        welfare,
Which speed we hope the better for our words...
Are they returned?
    Lorenzo.   Madam, they are not yet;
But there is come a messenger before,
To signify their coming.
    Portia.   Go in, Nerissa,
Give order to my servants that they take
No note at all of our being absent hence—
Nor you, Lorenzo—Jessica, nor you.
                    [*'a tucket sounds'; voices are heard
                        at a distance in the avenue*
    Lorenzo. Your husband is at hand, I hear
        his trumpet.
We are no tell-tales, madam—fear you not.
    Portia. This night methinks is but the daylight sick,
It looks a little paler—'tis a day,
Such as the day is when the sun is hid.

'BASSANIO, ANTONIO, GRATIANO, *and their followers*'
            come up

    Bassanio. We should hold day with the Antipodes,
If you would walk in absence of the sun.

Portia. Let me give light, but let me not be light,
For a light wife doth make a heavy husband,
And never be Bassanio so for me.
But God sort all....You are welcome home, my lord.
                    [*Gratiano and Nerissa talk apart*
Bassanio. I thank you, madam. Give welcome to
    my friend—
This is the man, this is Antonio,
To whom I am so infinitely bound.
  Portia. You should in all sense be much bound
    to him,
For, as I hear, he was much bound for you.
  Antonio. No more than I am well acquitted of.
  Portia. Sir, you are very welcome to our house:
It must appear in other ways than words,
Therefore I scant this breathing courtesy.
  Gratiano. By yonder moon I swear you do me wrong,
In faith I gave it to the judge's clerk.
Would he were gelt that had it for my part,
Since you do take it, love, so much at heart.
  Portia. A quarrel, ho, already! what's the matter?
  Gratiano. About a hoop of gold, a paltry ring
That she did give to me, whose posy was
For all the world like cutler's poetry
Upon a knife, 'Love me, and leave me not.'
  Nerissa. What talk you of the posy or the value?
You swore to me when I did give it you
That you would wear it till your hour of death,
And that it should lie with you in your grave.
Though not for me, yet for your vehement oaths,
You should have been respective and have kept it.
Gave it a judge's clerk! no, God's my judge,
The clerk will ne'er wear hair on's face that had it.
  Gratiano. He will, an if he live to be a man.

Nerissa. Ay, if a woman live to be a man.

Gratiano. Now, by this hand, I gave it to a youth,
A kind of boy, a little scrubbéd boy,
No higher than thyself, the judge's clerk,
A prating boy, that begged it as a fee—
I could not for my heart deny it him.

Portia. You were to blame, I must be plain
    with you,
To part so slightly with your wife's first gift,
A thing stuck on with oaths upon your finger,
†And riveted with faith unto your flesh.
I gave my love a ring, and made him swear
Never to part with it, and here he stands;
I dare be sworn for him he would not leave it,
Nor pluck it from his finger, for the wealth
That the world masters....Now, in faith, Gratiano,
You give your wife too unkind cause of grief.
An 'twere to me, I should be mad at it.

(*Bassanio.* Why, I were best to cut my left hand off,
And swear I lost the ring defending it.

Gratiano. My Lord Bassanio gave his ring away
Unto the judge that begged it, and indeed
Deserved it too; and then the boy, his clerk,
That took some pains in writing, he begged mine,
And neither man nor master would take aught
But the two rings.

Portia.   What ring gave you, my lord?
Not that, I hope, which you received of me.

Bassanio. If I could add a lie unto a fault,
I would deny it; but you see my finger
Hath not the ring upon it, it is gone.

Portia. Even so void is your false heart of truth....

                              [*she turns away*
By heaven, I will ne'er come in your bed

Until I see the ring.

Nerissa.   Nor I in yours,
Till I again see mine.

Bassanio.   Sweet Portia,
If you did know to whom I gave the ring,
If you did know for whom I gave the ring,
And would conceive for what I gave the ring,
And how unwillingly I left the ring,
When naught would be accepted but the ring,
You would abate the strength of your displeasure.

Portia. If you had known the virtue of the ring,
Or half her worthiness that gave the ring,
Or your own honour to contain the ring,
You would not then have parted with the ring...
What man is there so much unreasonable,
If you had pleased to have defended it
With any terms of zeal, wanted the modesty
To urge the thing held as a ceremony?
Nerissa teaches me what to believe—
I'll die for't but some woman had the ring.

Bassanio. No, by my honour, madam, by my soul,
No woman had it, but a civil doctor,
Which did refuse three thousand ducats of me,
And begged the ring, the which I did deny him,
And suffered him to go displeased away,
Even he that had held up the very life
Of my dear friend....What should I say, sweet lady?
I was enforced to send it after him,
I was beset with shame and courtesy,
My honour would not let ingratitude
So much besmear it...Pardon me, good lady,
For by these blesséd candles of the night,
Had you been there, I think you would have begged
The ring of me to give the worthy doctor.

Portia. Let not that doctor e'er come near my house.
Since he hath got the jewel that I loved,
And that which you did swear to keep for me,
I will become as liberal as you,
I'll not deny him any thing I have,
No, not my body, nor my husband's bed:
Know him I shall, I am well sure of it.
Lie not a night from home. Watch me, like Argus.
If you do not, if I be left alone,
Now, by mine honour, which is yet mine own,
I'll have that doctor for my bedfellow.

Nerissa. And I his clerk; therefore be well advised
How you do leave me to mine own protection.

Gratiano. Well, do you so: let not me take him then,
For if I do, I'll mar the young clerk's pen.

Antonio. I am th'unhappy subject of these quarrels.

Portia. Sir, grieve not you—you are welcome
    notwithstanding.

Bassanio. Portia, forgive me this enforcéd wrong,
And in the hearing of these many friends
I swear to thee, even by thine own fair eyes
Wherein I see myself—

Portia.   Mark you but that!
In both my eyes he doubly sees himself:
In each eye, one. Swear by your double self,
And there's an oath of credit.

Bassanio.   Nay, but hear me....
Pardon this fault, and by my soul I swear,
I never more will break an oath with thee.

Antonio. I once did lend my body for his wealth,
Which but for him that had your husband's ring
Had quite miscarried. I dare be bound again,
My soul upon the forfeit, that your lord
Will never more break faith advisedly.

Portia. Then you shall be his surety....[*she takes a ring from her finger*] Give him this,
And bid him keep it better than the other.
  Antonio. Here, Lord Bassanio, swear to keep this ring.
  Bassanio. By heaven, it is the same I gave the doctor!
  Portia. I had it of him: pardon me, Bassanio,
For by this ring the doctor lay with me.
  Nerissa [*shows a ring also*]. And pardon me, my
     gentle Gratiano,
For that same scrubbéd boy, the doctor's clerk,
In lieu of this last night did lie with me.
  Gratiano. Why, this is like the mending of highways
In summer, where the ways are fair enough.
What! are we cuckolds ere we have deserved it?
  Portia. Speak not so grossly. You are all amazed:
Here is a letter, read it at your leisure—
It comes from Padua, from Bellario.
There you shall find that Portia was the doctor,
Nerissa there, her clerk...Lorenzo here
Shall witness I set forth as soon as you,
And even but now returned; I have not yet
Entered my house....Antonio, you are welcome,
And I have better news in store for you
Than you expect: unseal this letter soon,
There you shall find three of your argosies
Are richly come to harbour suddenly....
You shall not know by what strange accident
I chancéd on this letter.
  Antonio.   I am dumb!
  Bassanio. Were you the doctor, and I knew you not?
  Gratiano. Were you the clerk that is to make
     me cuckold?
  Nerissa. Ay, but the clerk that never means to do it,
Unless he live until he be a man.

Bassanio. Sweet doctor, you shall be my bedfellow—
When I am absent, then lie with my wife.
  Antonio. Sweet lady, you have given me life
    and living;
For here I read for certain that my ships
Are safely come to road.
  Portia.   How now, Lorenzo?
My clerk hath some good comforts too for you.
  Nerissa. Ay, and I'll give them him without a fee....
There do I give to you and Jessica,
From the rich Jew, a special deed of gift,
After his death, of all he dies possessed of.
  Lorenzo. Fair ladies, you drop manna in the way
Of starvéd people.
  Portia.   It is almost morning,
And yet I am sure you are not satisfied
Of these events at full. Let us go in,
And charge us there upon inter'gatories,
And we will answer all things faithfully.
  Gratiano. Let it be so. The first inter'gatory
That my Nerissa shall be sworn on is,
Whether till the next night she had rather stay,
Or go to bed now, being two hours to-day:
But were the day come, I should wish it dark,
Till I were couching with the doctor's clerk....
Well, while I live I'll fear no other thing
So sore as keeping safe Nerissa's ring.   *[they all go in*

GLOSSARY

Note. Where a pun or quibble is intended, the meanings are distinguished as (*a*) and (*b*)

ABODE, delay; 2. 6. 21

ADDRESS, prepare (cf. *Wint.* 4. 4. 53 'Address yourself to entertain them sprightly'); 2. 9. 19

ADVICE, 'upon more advice,' i.e. upon further consideration; 4. 2. 6

ADVISE, consider, reflect; 1. 1. 142; 2. 1. 42

AFFECTION, disposition, inclination (of the mind or body); 1. 1. 16; 3. 1. 55; 4. 1. 50

ANGEL, 'an old English gold coin... having as its device the archangel Michael standing upon and piercing the dragon' (N.E.D.), value about 10*s.*; 2. 7. 56

APPROPRIATION, special attribute; 1. 2. 39

APPROVE, make good, justify; 3. 2. 79

ARGOSY, 'a merchant-vessel of the largest size and burden; esp. those of Ragusa and Venice' (N.E.D.). The word is a corruption of 'Aragouse,' the 16th cent. form of 'Ragusa' (cf. *Sh. Eng.* i. 153); 1. 1. 9

ASPECT, appearance; 1. 1. 54; 2. 1. 8

ASSUME, 'to take to oneself formally the insignia of office or symbol of a vocation' (N.E.D.); 2. 9. 51

ATTENTIVE, observant; 5. 1. 71

BANE, poison; 4. 1. 46

BATE, depress, reduce in weight; 3. 3. 32

BLACK-MONDAY, i.e. Easter Monday, the 'movable' day, as Lancelot implies; 2. 5. 25

BLUNT, (*a*) unceremonious, (*b*) not to be sharpened (in reference to lead); 2. 7. 8

BOTTOM, hull; 1. 1. 42

BREAK, i.e. break faith, break his day; 1. 3. 133

BREAK UP, to open a letter (i.e. break the wax); 2. 4. 11

CARRION, (i) putrefying; 4. 1. 41; (ii) like a skeleton from which the flesh has rotted away; 2. 7. 63; 3. 1. 33

CATER-COUSIN, 'scarce cater-cousins,' i.e. hardly on speaking terms. The derivation of 'cater' is obscure; N.E.D. is inclined to interpret the phrase as 'originally those who were "cousins" by being catered for or boarded together,' a meaning which would be very apt in the present instance. In Eliz. English, of course, 'cousin' often meant little more than 'acquaintance'; 2. 2. 129

CERECLOTH, winding-sheet (lit. a cloth dipped in melted wax); 2. 7. 51

CHEER, face, countenance (the orig. meaning); 3. 2. 313

CHOOSE! do as you please! take your own way! (in mod. slang 'lump it'); v. N.E.D. 4 *b*; 1. 2. 45

CIRCUMSTANCE, circumlocution (cf. *Two Gent.* 1. 1. 36, 37); 1. 1. 154

CLOSE, secret; 2. 6. 47

COLD, 'without power to move or influence' (N.E.D. doubtfully); cf. *Two Gent.* 4. 4. 179 'I hope my master's suit will be but cold'; 2. 7. 73

COLT, 'a young or inexperienced person' (N.E.D.); 1. 2. 38

COMING-IN, 'a simple coming-in,' i.e. a poor allowance (prob. with an indelicate secondary meaning; cf. *Gen.* xix. 31); 2. 2. 161

COMMODITY, (i) goods; 1. 1. 178; (ii) advantage, privileges; 3. 3. 27

COMPLEXION, disposition, nature; 3. 1. 28

COMPROMISED (to be), come to terms, settle differences; 1. 3. 75

CONCEIT, conception, understanding; 3. 4. 2

CONDITION, disposition, character; 1. 2. 124

CONDITIONED, 'best conditioned' = best tempered, 3. 2. 294

CONSTANT, resolute, self-possessed; 3. 2. 248

CONTAIN, retain, keep in one's possession or under one's control; 4. 1. 50; 5. 1. 202

CONTINENT, 'that which comprises or sums up, the sum and substance' (N.E.D.); 3. 2. 130

COPE. There are two distinct verbs, 'cope,' meaning (i) strike, encounter, have to do with; and (ii) buy, barter, give in exchange for. Shakespeare is not exactly quibbling here, but he seems to have both meanings in mind; 4. 1. 408

COVER, (*a*) lay the cloth, (*b*) cover the head; 3. 5. 47, 49

CRISPÉD, closely and stiffly curled; 3. 2. 92

CURTSY, (*a*) polite bow (not, as now, confined to feminine genuflexion), (*b*) a small quantity, a trifle (cf. mod. idiom 'a nodding acquaintance with'); 3. 1. 46

DANGER, 'within his danger,' i.e.

in his power, at his mercy (orig. meaning of 'danger' was 'lordship, sovereignty'); 4. 1. 177

DEATH, skull (cf. *L.L.L.* 5. 2. 610); 2. 7. 63

DISABLE, disparage (cf. *A.Y.L.* 4. 1. 34 'disable all the benefits of your own country'); 2. 7. 30

DISCHARGE, pay (a debt), cf. *Errors*, 4. 1. 13 'I will discharge my bond'; 4. 1. 205

DISCOVER, to reveal by drawing aside a curtain. A technical term of the theatre (cf. *Temp.* 5. 1. 72 S.D.; Chambers, *Eliz. Stage*, iii. 81–2); 2. 7. 1

DISCRETION, discrimination; 3. 5. 60

DISH OF DOVES, i.e. enough doves to fill a dish when cooked; 2. 2. 134

DOIT, 'a small Dutch coin formerly in use...the half of an English farthing...a very small or trifling sum' (N.E.D.); 1.3.137

DUCAT, a Spanish gold coin, valued under Philip and Mary at 6*s.* 8*d.*, the 'double ducat' being worth 13*s.* 4*d.* (v. *Sh. Eng.* i. 342); 1. 3. 1, etc.

DUMB-SHOW, a silent performance of part of a play, intended either to explain briefly the events that pass between two acts, or to foreshadow in emblematic fashion what is to follow; 1. 2. 69

EANLING, new-born lamb; 1. 3. 76

EGALL, equal (the form also occurs in *Titus*, 4. 4. 4, and *R. III*, 3. 7. 213); 3. 4. 13

EKE, add to, lengthen, increase; 3. 2. 23

ELECTION, making a choice; 2. 9. 3; 3. 2. 24

EREBUS, the classical hell; 5. 1. 88

EVEN, impartial; 2. 7. 25

EXCREMENT, any outgrowth of the body, e.g. hair, nails; 3. 2. 87

FANCY, inclination, baseless supposition, fantasy (of which word it was orig. a contraction); 3. 2. 63, 68, 70

FIA, mispronunciation of 'via' (q.v.); 2. 2. 10

FILL-HORSE, cart-horse. The 'fills' or 'thrills' were the shafts of a cart; 2. 2. 92

FIND FORTH, find out (cf. *Err.* 1. 2. 37; *Two Gent.* 2. 4. 184); 1. 1. 143

FLEDGE, an obs. form of 'fledged'; 3. 1. 28

FLIGHT, 'of the self-same flight' = of the same carrying power. A flight really consisted of 'two or three arrows, matched and found to fly exactly alike' (*Sh. Eng.* ii. 381); 1. 1. 141

FOND, foolish; 3. 3. 9

FULSOME, rank; 1. 3. 83

GABERDINE, a loose upper garment of coarse material (cf. *Temp.* 2. 2. 40); 1. 3. 109

GAGED, pledged; 1. 1. 130

GAPING PIG, a pig's-head, with its mouth open, prepared for the table. Malone quotes Nashe, *Pierce Penilesse*, 1592, 'Some will take on like a madman if they see a pigge come to the table' (v. McKerrow, *Nashe*, i. 188), and observes that this passage 'perhaps furnished our author with his instance'; 4. 1. 47, 54

GARNISH, outfit, garment; 2. 6. 45

GARNISHED, furnished. Most edd. interpret 'furnished with words'; but surely the meaning is 'with the fool's outfit of motley, cap and bauble'; 3. 5. 64

GEAR, purpose, business; 1. 1. 110; 2. 2. 165

GLEAN, (*a*) glean corn, (*b*) cut off

stragglers in battle (cf. 'low peasantry'), N.E.D. 'glean' 3 *d*; 2. 9. 46

GOODLY, gracious, benign; 3. 5. 45

GRAVEL-BLIND, a jocular link between 'Sand-blind' (q.v.) and Stone-blind; 2. 2. 33

GROW TO, 'a household phrase applied to milk when burnt to the bottom of the saucepan and thence acquiring an unpleasant taste' (Clark and Wright); 2. 2. 16

GUARDED, ornamented with trimming or lace; 2. 2. 154

GUILÉD, treacherous, endowed with guiles (cf. 'delighted,' *Meas.* 3. 1. 120); 3. 2. 97

HEARSED, coffined; 3. 1. 82

HEAVENS (for the), in heaven's name; 2. 2. 11

HIGH-DAY, holiday (cf. *Temp.* 2. 2. 191); 2. 9. 98

HIP (to have upon), a wrestling metaphor (cf. *Sh. Hand*, pp. 165–66); 1. 3. 43; 4. 1. 330

HOVEL-POST, a post used in the making of a stack of corn (v. N.E.D. 'hovel' 4); 2. 2. 64

HUMILITY, humanity (cf. *L.L.L.* 4. 3. 346 'plant in tyrants mild humility'; *Hen. V*, 3. 1. 4; *R. III*, 2. 1. 72); N.E.D. does not notice this meaning, which seems to be restricted to Shakespeare; 3. 1. 64

HUSBANDRY, administration of the household; 3. 4. 25

HYRCANIA, the land south of the Caspian Sea, proverbial for wildness and savagery; 2. 7. 41

IMPEACH, discredit, call in question; 3. 2. 279; 3. 3. 29

IMPOSITION, command, charge laid upon one; 1. 2. 99; 3. 4. 33

IMPUGN, dispute the validity of a statement or line of action; 4. 1. 176

INCISION (make), let blood. A technical expression in surgery. (Cf. *L.L.L.* 4. 3. 94 and Jonson, *Cynthia's Revels*, 4. 1., which speaks of a lover 'stabbing himself, drinking healths, or writing languishing letters in his blood'); 2. 1. 6

INFECTION, blunder for 'affection'; 2. 2. 123

INSCULPED, engraved; 2. 7. 57

INTER'GATORY. A reference to Chancery jurisdiction of the period, which 'got at the truth by putting searching interrogations to the defendant himself which he had to answer on oath, and by clapping him in prison if he disobeyed the Chancellor's orders' (*Sh. Eng.* i. 395); 5. 1. 299, 301

INTERMISSION, pastime, lit. a rest during a period of work; 3. 2. 200

JACK, knave; 3. 4. 77

JEW'S EYE, a proverbial expression for something valued highly (cf. G. Harvey, 1592, 'A souerain Rule, as deare as a Iewes eye'); 2. 5. 42

KNAP, to bite with a crackling sound; 3. 1. 9

LEAVE, part with, lose (N.E.D. 8 *b*); 5. 1. 151, 173, 197

LEVEL AT, aim at, guess at (lit. to aim with a bow or gun); 1. 2. 36

LICHAS, the servant of Hercules who unwittingly brought his master the Nessus shirt; 2. 1. 32

LIEU, 'in lieu of,' i.e. as a payment for, as a reward for, in acknowledgment of; 4. 1. 406; 5. 1. 263

LIGHT, loose; 2. 6. 42; 5. 1. 130

LIKELY, comely; 2. 9. 92

LIVERY, the badge or cognizance worn by the retainers of some great lord (cf. *shadowed*); 2. 1. 2

MAGNIFICO, Venetian grandee; 3. 2. 281; 4. 1. S.D. head

MANTLE, 'of liquids: to become covered with a coating or scum' (N.E.D.); 1. 1. 89

MARK, 'God bless the mark!' N.E.D. explains as 'an exclamatory phrase, prob. originally serving as a formula to avert an evil omen and hence used by way of apology when something horrible, disgusting, indecent or profane has been mentioned' (cf. *Two Gent.* 4. 4. 18); 2. 2. 22

MERE, sheer, complete; 3. 2. 263

MIND OF LOVE, i.e. love-schemes; 'mind' = purpose, resolution; 2. 8. 42

MO, more in number. Formerly 'more' meant 'more in quantity' only; 4. 1. 81

MOIETY, share, portion (lit. half); 4. 1. 26

MORTAL-BREATHING, i.e. like a mortal, breathing (and yet a saint); 2. 7. 40

MORTIFYING, death-causing. Sighs and groans were supposed to drain the blood (cf. *M.D.N.* 3. 2. 97 note); 1. 1. 82

MOTION, inward prompting or impulse, desire, inclination, emotion; 5. 1. 87

MUTUAL, common to more than two. Much more frequently used by Shakespeare in this than in what is now regarded as the only correct sense; 5. 1. 78

NAUGHTY, wicked, good for naught; 3. 3. 9; 5. 1. 92

NEAT'S TONGUE, i.e. a cured or dried ox-tongue; 1. 1. 112

OBLIGÉD FAITH, 'faith bound by contract' (Aldis Wright); 2. 6. 7

OCCASION, i.e. events as they fall out; 3. 5. 51

OFFENCE, displeasure, annoyance (v. N.E.D. 5*b*); 4. 1. 68

OFFICER, a sheriff's officer, catch-pole (cf. *Err.* G. 'sergeant of the band'); 3. 1. 118

OLD. Colloquial, meaning 'plenti-ful, great'; 4. 2. 15

OPINION, reputation; 1. 1. 91, 102

OSTENT, show, display; 2. 2. 193; 2. 8. 44

O'ER-LOOK. A technical term in witchcraft, meaning ' look upon one with the evil eye' (cf. 'be-shrew your eyes'); 3. 2. 15

OVERPEER, tower above; 1. 1. 12

OVER-WEATHERED, worn by ex-posure to the weather (N.E.D. quotes no other instance); 2. 6. 18

PAGEANT, a movable scaffold on which open-air scenes were enacted or tableaux displayed in the miracle play and civic show (a very apt simile for the Eliza-bethan argosy); 1. 1. 11

PARCEL, lot, set (contemptuous); 1. 2. 103

PART, depart; 2. 7. 77

PASSION, bodily disorder; 4. 1. 51

PATEN, the small flat dish used with the chalice in the adminis-tration of Holy Communion; 5. 1. 60

PAWN, stake, wager; 3. 5. 77

PEEVISH, morose. 'In early quota-tions often referred to as the result of religious austerities, fasting and the like' (N.E.D.); 1. 1. 86

PEISE THE TIME, (i) 'weigh with deliberation each precious mo-ment' (Clark and Wright), (ii) 'weight the time that it may pass slowly' (Steevens). Which-ever interpretation we adopt, Shakespeare used the word 'peise' because of its technical associations with the clock, 'peise' being the regular name for the weights used in winding; 3. 2. 22

PENT-HOUSE, v. note; 2. 6. 1

PICK, select, pick out carefully; 2. 9. 48

PILL, peel, strip (v. note); 1. 3. 81

PIRE, peer, examine closely. The form 'peer' is not found before 1590; cf. note; 1. 1. 19

PORT, grand or expensive style of living; 1. 1. 124

POSSESSED, informed; 1. 3. 61

POST, courier, messenger; 2. 9. 100

POSY, 'a short motto, originally a line of verse of poetry and usually in patterned language, inscribed on a knife, within a ring, as a heraldic motto, etc.' (N.E.D.); 5. 1. 149, 152

PRESENTLY, immediately; 1. 1. 183

PREST, ready; 1. 1. 160

PREVENT, forestall, anticipate; 1. 1. 61

PURCHASE, acquire, gain; 2. 9. 43

QUAINT, skilful, cunning, knowing; 2. 4. 6; 3. 4. 69

QUALIFY, moderate, temper; 4. 1. 7

QUALITY, (i) manner, style; 3. 2. 6; (ii) trait, human characteristic ('the quality of mercy' = the quality, mercy); 4. 1. 181

RACE, herd, stud; 5. 1. 73

RACK, stretch; 1. 1. 181

RATE, *sb.* style, mode of living; 1. 1. 127

RATE, *vb.* value; 2. 7. 26

REASON, talk, hold conversation with; 2. 8. 27

REED-VOICE, a reedy or squeaking voice (apparently a technical term in music, v. *Sh. Eng.* ii. 45); 3. 4. 67

REGREETS, salutations; 2. 9. 89

REHEARSE, mention, formally recite; 4. 1. 358

RESPECT (without), without reference to other things (cf. *Ham.* 2. 2. 255 'There is nothing either good or bad, but thinking makes it so'); 5. 1. 100

RESPECTIVE, careful, regardful; 5. 1. 157

REST, 'set up one's rest,' i.e. to be determined, resolved. The expression, derived from the card-game, primero, in which 'the rest' was the name for the reserved stakes, originally meant 'to hazard one's all'; 2. 2. 100

RHENISH, a white wine from the Rhine, such as hock or moselle; 1. 2. 91; 3. 1. 38

RIALTO, the name of the Exchange in Venice; 1. 3. 19, etc.

RIB, enclose; 2. 7. 51

ROAD, roadstead; 1. 1. 19

ROTH, obs. spelling of 'ruth' = calamity, grief (cf. note); 2. 9. 78

RUIN, rubbish, refuse; 2. 9. 48

SAD, sober, serious; 2. 2. 193

SAND-BLIND, partially blind, probably a perversion of the O.E. 'samblind' = half-blind (N.E.D.); 2. 2. 33, 71

SCANT, limit, restrict, cut short; 2. 1. 17; 5. 1. 142

SCARFÉD, decked with streamers; 2. 6. 15

SCRUBBÉD, undersized, insignificant; 5. 1. 163

SEASON, alleviate, temper (lit. to mix something with food to make it more palatable); 3. 2. 76; 4. 1. 194

SENSE (in all), on every account; 5. 1. 137

SENSIBLE, substantial, tangible; 2. 9. 89

SENTENCES, maxims; 1. 2. 9

SERVITOR, attendant (a theatrical term, v. note); 2. 9. S.D. head

SET FORTH, (*a*) extol, praise greatly, (*b*) serve up to the table (of dishes); 3. 5. 85

SET UP ONE'S REST, v. *rest*; 2. 2. 100

SHADOWED, shaded, umbrated (a heraldic term); 2. 1. 2

SHRINE, i.e. image of a saint or god. This sense not found outside Shakespeare (but cf. *Lucr.* 194, *Cymb.* 5. 5. 164); 2. 7. 40

SIBYLLA, the Sibyl of Cumae, keeper of the Sibylline books, to whom Apollo granted that her years should be as many as the grains in a handful of sand; 1. 2. 101

SIMPLE, poor, wretched, pitiful; 2. 2. 159, 161

SIMPLICITY, folly; 1. 3. 40

SINGLE BOND. Meaning doubtful; either (i) unconditional bond, or (ii) a bond without the names of the sureties attached; 1. 3. 142

SLIPS OF PROLIXITY, lapses into tediousness; 3. 1. 11

SLUBBER, perform in a slovenly manner (lit. daub); 2. 8. 39

SMACK, savour of, be strongly suggestive of (cf. *K. John*, 1. 1. 208–209); 2. 2. 16

SONTIES, saints—diminutive of 'sont,' an old form of 'saint'; 2. 2. 41

SOON AT, towards, near (of time); 2. 3. 5

SOPHY, formerly a title of the Shah of Persia (1500–1736); 2. 1. 25

SORT, *sb.* manner, method; 1. 2. 99

SORT, *vb.* ordain, dispose (cf. *R. III*, 2. 3. 36 'if God sort it so'); 5. 1. 133

SPIRITS, 'faculties of perception' (N.E.D. 18); 5. 1. 71

SUFFICIENT, substantial, well-to-do, financially sound; 1. 3. 17, 25

SULTAN SOLYMAN, Solyman the Magnificent, Sultan of Turkey 1490–1566, who in 1535 undertook a campaign against the Persians; 2. 1. 26

TABLE. In palmistry the 'table' is the quadrangular space formed by the four principal 'lines' in the palm of the hand; 2. 2. 157

TERMS, 'in terms of,' in respect of; 2. 1. 13

THRIFT, (i) thriving, success; 1. 1. 175; (ii) gain, profit; 1. 3. 47, 87

TIME, time of life, age (here 'youth'); 1. 1. 129

TOUCH, note, strain (lit. the fingering of the instrument); 5. 1. 58

TUCKET, a flourish on a trumpet; 5. 1. 122 S.D.

TURN TO. (Cf. *M.W.W.* 2. 1. 164 'turn her loose to him,' 168 'turn them together' and *Temp.* 2. 1. 124 note); 1. 3. 78; 3. 4. 78

TYRANNY, cruelty; 4. 1. 13

UNBATED, unabated; 2. 6. 11

UNFURNISHED, unprovided with its fellow; 3. 2. 126

UNHANDLED, not broken in; 5. 1. 73

UNTREAD, retrace; 2. 6. 10

VAIL, lower; 1. 1. 28

VANTAGE, opportunity (Portia is thinking of some game or contest); 3. 2. 175

VENDIBLE, 'a maid not vendible,' i.e. an old maid past marriageable age (lit. past her market); 1. 1. 112

VENTURE, commercial speculation (cf. *Sh.Eng.* i. 334); 1. 1. 15, 21, 42; 1. 3. 20

VIA, 'an adverb of encouraging much used by commanders, as also by riders to their horses' (Florio). Lancelot pronounces the word 'Fia'; 2. 2. 10

WARRANTY, authorisation; 1. 1. 132

WELL TO LIVE, in capital health (cf. 'well-to-do'); 2. 2. 49

WIND ABOUT. A metaphor from stalking game: we should say 'beat about the bush'; 1. 1. 154

YOUNGER, the younger son of the parable (cf. *Luke* xv. 12). Rowe read 'younker' (cf. *3 Hen. VI*, 2. 1. 24 'trimmed like a younker prancing to his love'); the meaning is the same, and it is clear from *1 Hen. IV*, 3. 3. 92 that 'younker' was simply another name for the Prodigal Son; 2. 6. 14

YOUNG-EYED, i.e. with sight ever young. Mediaeval tradition endowed the Cherubim with a peculiar power of seeing, and in the three other places where Shakespeare mentions them the notion of keen sight is introduced (cf. *Ham.* 4. 3. 50; *Macb.* 1. 7. 22–4; *Troil.* 3. 2. 74–5). We are indebted to Verity for this note; 5. 1. 63

WORDSWORTH CLASSICS

General Editors: Marcus Clapham and Clive Reynard
Titles in this series

Pride and Prejudice

Wuthering Heights

Alice in Wonderland

Father Brown: Selected Stories

Great Expectations

Tess of the d'Urbervilles

A Portrait of the Artist

Women in Love

Moby Dick

Hamlet

Twelfth Night

Tom Sawyer & Huckleberry Finn

The Last of the Mohicans

Oliver Twist

Romeo and Juliet

The Picture of Dorian Gray

Sense and Sensibility

The Wind in the Willows

Othello

Vanity Fair

Jane Eyre

Tom Jones

Ghost Stories

Julius Caesar

David Copperfield

The Odyssey

Call of the Wild & White Fang

Gulliver's Travels

Emma

The Scarlet Letter

A Midsummer Night's Dream

20,000 Leagues Under the Sea

Mansfield Park

The Adventures of Sherlock Holmes

The Ambassadors

Macbeth

Don Quixote

The Riddle of the Sands

Dracula

A Tale of Two Cities

Northanger Abbey

The Three Musketeers

The Great Gatsby

Richard II

The Moonstone

Robinson Crusoe

Cranford

Sons and Lovers

Lord Jim

Three Men in a Boat

Dubliners

Tales of Mystery and Imagination

Pickwick Papers

Plain Tales from the Hills

Richard III

Frankenstein

Persuasion

Memoirs of a Woman of
Pleasure: Fanny Hill

The Return of Sherlock Holmes

As You Like It

The Merchant of Venice

Dr Jekyll and Mr Hyde

War and Peace

Candide

Shirley

Secret Agent

Far from the Madding Crowd

Lord Arthur Savile's Crime &
Other Stories

The Case-Book of Sherlock
Holmes

The Hunchback of Notre Dame

The Turn of the Screw & The
Aspern Papers

The Complete Stories of Saki

Villette

Moll Flanders

The Mill on the Floss

Antony and Cleopatra

Lorna Doone

The Woman in White

Madame Bovary

The Taming of the Shrew

The Thirty-nine Steps

Hadrian the VII

Bleak House

Troilus and Cressida

The Red Badge of Courage

Nicholas Nickleby

Les Miserables

The Warden

Henry V

Barchester Towers

Around the World in 80 Days &
5 Weeks in a Balloon

To the Lighthouse

The Tenant of Wildfell Hall

North and South

Raffles: The Amateur Cracksman

King Lear

Confessions of an English Opium
Eater

Tender is the Night

The Mayor of Casterbridge

Kim

Crime and Punishment

Diary of a Nobody

Ivanhoe

The Tempest

Distribution

AUSTRALIA, BRUNEI
& MALAYSIA
Reed Editions
22 Salmon Street, Port Melbourne
Vic 3207, Australia
Tel: (03) 646 6716
Fax (03) 646 6925

DENMARK
BOG-FAN
St. Kongensgade 61A
1264 København K

BOGPA SIKA
Industrivej 1, 7120 Vejle Ø

FRANCE
Bookking International
16 Rue des Grands Augustins
75006 Paris

GERMANY, AUSTRIA
& SWITZERLAND
Swan Buch-Marketing GmbH
Goldscheuerstrabe 16
D-7640 Kehl Am Rhein, Germany

GREAT BRITAIN & IRELAND
Wordsworth Editions Ltd
Cumberland House, Crib Street,
Ware, Hertfordshire SG12 9ET

Selecta Books
The Selectabook
Distribution Centre
Folly Road, Roundway, Devizes
Wiltshire SN10 2HR

HOLLAND & BELGIUM
Uitgeverlj en Boekhandel
Van Gennep BV, Spuistraat 283
1012 VR Amsterdam, Holland

INDIA
OM Book Service
1690 First Floor
Nai Sarak, Delhi – 110006
Tel: 3279823-3265303 Fax: 3278091

ITALY
Magis Books
Piazza Della Vittoria l/C
42100 Reggio Emilia
Tel: 0522-452303 Fax: 0522-452845

NEW ZEALAND
Whitcoulls Limited
Private Bag 92098, Auckland

NORWAY
Norsk Bokimport AS
Bertrand Narvesensvei 2
Postboks 6219, Etterstad, 0602 Oslo

PORTUGAL
Cashkeen Limited
(Isabel Leao) 25 Elmhurst Avenue
London N2 0LT
Tel: 081-444 3781 Fax: 081-444 3171

SINGAPORE
Book Station
18 Leo Drive, Singapore
Tel: 4511998 Fax: 4529188

SOUTH EAST CYPRUS
Tinkerbell Books
19 Dimitri Hamatsou Street, Paralimni
Famagusta, Cyprus
Tel: 03-8200 75

SOUTH WEST CYPRUS & GREECE
Huckleberry Trading
4 Isabella, Anavargos, Pafos, Cyprus
Tel: 06-231313

SOUTH AFRICA, ZIMBABWE
CENTRAL & E. AFRICA
Trade Winds Press (Pty) Ltd
P O Box 20194, Durban North 4016

SPAIN
Ribera Libros
Dr. Areilza No.19, 48011 Bilbao
Tel: 441-87-87 Fax: 441-80-29

USA, CANADA & MEXICO
Universal Sales & Marketing
230 Fifth Avenue, Suite 1212
New York, N Y 10001 USA
Tel: 212-481-3500 Fax: 212-481-3534

DIRECT MAIL
Redvers
Redvers House, 13 Fairmile,
Henley-on-Thames, Oxfordshire RG9 2JR
Tel: 0491 572656 Fax: 0491 573590